Cooking School

CHINESE

Cooking School

CHINESE

Bring the flavors of China to life in your own kitchen!

This edition published in 2010
LOVE FOOD is an imprint of Parragon Books Ltd

Parragon
Queen Street House
4 Queen Street
Bath BA1 1HE, UK

ISBN: 978-1-4075-9477-4

Printed in China

Internal design by Pink Creative
Internal photography by Charlie Richards*
Internal food styling by Anna Burges-Lumsden
Internal prop styling by Sarah Waller
Introduction by Christine McFadden

Notes for the Reader

This book uses imperial, metric, and US cup measurements. Follow the same units of measurement throughout; do not mix imperial and metric. All spoon measurements are level: teaspoons are assumed to be 5 ml, and tablespoons are assumed to be 15 ml. Unless otherwise stated, milk is assumed to be whole, eggs and individual vegetables, such as potatoes, are medium, and pepper is freshly ground black pepper.

Recipes using raw or very lightly cooked eggs should be avoided by infants, the elderly, pregnant women, convalescents, and anyone with a chronic condition. Pregnant and breastfeeding women are advised to avoid eating peanuts and peanut products. People with nut allergies should be aware that some of the prepared ingredients used in the recipes in this book may contain nuts. Always check the packaging before use.

* except pages 16, 40, 48, 60, 63, 72, 76, 79, 83, 84, 88, 91, 92, 96, 103, 112, 115, 119, 120, 131, 136, 144, 159, 160, 168, 171 & 172

Contents

Introduction

Mastering the basics of Chinese cooking will give you a marvelous opportunity to explore not only the fabulous array of ingredients, the all-important preparation techniques, and the different cooking methods, but also to go deeper into the history, geography, and culture that lie behind Chinese regional cuisines. Armed with this knowledge, you will be amazed at the ease with which you can create an impressive range of dishes in your own kitchen, whether it's a multi-dish Chinese meal or a simple accompaniment to your normal menu.

Regional Cooking

China is as vast as the United States, spanning many degrees of latitude. It has radical variations in climate, ranging from year-round subarctic conditions in the north, to the sweltering tropics of the southern coastal regions. China's topography is equally extreme. From the Tibetan Plateau in the northwest (11,800 ft/3,600 m) the land descends in a series of steps to the fertile coastal plains in the east and south. It is this diversity of topography and climate that lie behind the intriguing variations of regional cooking.

Peking (Northern Cuisine)

The food in this region relies on staples, such as wheat, sorghum, millet, and soybeans. Wheat is a major crop, which means that noodles are the order of the day rather than rice. The food tends to be homely and robust, although the well-known Peking Duck is an exception. Hearty lamb dishes are popular, such as Lamb with Black Bean Sauce, reflecting the influence of Chinese Muslims who, for religious reasons, eat lamb instead of pork.

Canton (Southern Cuisine)

Cantonese cuisine offers an astonishing melting pot of culinary feasts and is renowned for top-notch seafood, fresh fruit and vegetables, stunning stir-fries, and dim sum to die for. Considered the gold standard of Chinese cuisine, Cantonese food is the best known in the Western world, thanks to the large numbers of Chinese who emigrated to Europe and the United States in the nineteenth century. Cantonese dishes, such as Sweet-and-Sour Pork and Sweet-and-Sour Spareribs, are well known the world over.

Because Canton was the first Chinese trading port, the region is greatly influenced by foreign contact. For example, broccoli and asparagus were introduced from abroad and were popular in Canton before being taken up elsewhere. Cooking with fruit and fruit-based sauces, as in Fruity Duck Stir-Fry, is also typical of the region. Seasonings are typically kept light, with limited use of soy sauce, in order to let the ingredients shine.

Shanghai (Eastern Cuisine)

Based around the Chang Delta, this fertile region produces both rice and wheat as well as an abundance of fruit and vegetables. Fresh fish comes not only from the sea but also from the numerous lakes and rivers that crisscross the land. Perhaps least known in the West, Shanghai cuisine is a mixture of styles, characterized by rich complex flavors and the lavish use of the rich soy sauce for which the Chang Delta is renowned. Sugar is also a key ingredient, especially in salty dishes in which it balances flavor without introducing obvious sweetness.

Sichuan (Western Cuisine)

Known in China as "the land of plenty," Sichuan enjoys rich, fertile soil, a warm climate, and copious rainfall. The region produces an enormous variety of fruit, vegetables, fungi, and fish, which are put to good use in richly flavored, heavily sauced dishes.

Sichuan cuisine has much more to offer than the hot and spicy dishes for which it is famous in the West. Although chiles and pepper are certainly used as "warming" foods to counteract the region's inherent dampness, these pungent seasonings are never used in a way that overwhelms other ingredients. Delicately flavored bamboo shoots and tofu feature in the cuisine, and in restaurants "cool" and "medium" dishes as well as "hot" ones are usually on the menu. The region is also noted for pickled or dry-salted vegetables.

Cooking and Eating Styles

For the Chinese, food and its supply have always been of vital concern; it is deeply appreciated and nothing is ever wasted. Regardless of the region, food is prepared, cooked, and served in accordance with the age-old Taoist principles of Yin and Yang, in which balance and contrast are key. Some of the ingredients and cooking methods may vary from one region to another, but basically all dishes are unmistakably "Chinese."

What distinguishes Chinese food is the emphasis on harmonious blending of color, texture, aroma, and flavor, both in a single dish and in the dishes that make up the meal. Of great importance is "fire control," as the Chinese call it; there are at least 40 different methods of heating food! Understanding basics, such as preheating a wok until almost red hot, will help you to achieve the necessary texture, whether crisp or soft, wet or dry, or slippery or crunchy.

Timing is equally important. If the heat is sufficiently high, food will cook quickly, but beginners tend to make the mistake of cooking food for too long over too low a heat.

Also important are the size and the shape of the prepared ingredient; this must be appropriate for a particular method of cooking. For example, food for quick stir-frying is cut into small, thin slices of uniform size, and never into large chunks. This is not only for appearance's sake, but also because ingredients of the same size and shape cook in the same amount of time.

Chinese Meals and Snacks

Day-to-day meals eaten at home are usually fairly simple, although made up of a variety of dishes. The meal is served all at once, in contrast to a formal banquet where dishes are served in a prescribed sequence. Unlike Western convention, dishes are never allocated to individual diners; everything on the table is shared. The Chinese do not usually finish a meal with a dessert, although sweet dishes might punctuate a full-scale banquet and fruit might be served at the end of a multicourse restaurant meal. Sweet dishes are usually eaten between meals as snacks.

Snacking and street food play a big part in Chinese culture. The Chinese love to buy all kinds of tasty snacks that are freshly cooked at roadside stalls, eating them on the run as they go about their daily life. In the evening, the sidewalks are filled with groups of families and friends cooking, selling, and sharing delicious food. Living in overcrowded conditions as many Chinese do, getting together in this way is an important and enjoyable part of social life.

Menu Planning

For a shared meal allow one dish per person. For example, if cooking for only two or three people, serve one main dish with a vegetable side dish and a rice or noodle dish, plus a soup if you like. For an informal meal for four to six people, serve four dishes plus soup and rice; for a formal dinner for the same number, allow six to eight dishes. When cooking for large numbers, always increase the number of dishes instead of the quantity of ingredients. That way, you'll have more variety of flavor, color, and texture.

Fundamental Techniques

Chopping

Cut the ingredients into small, equal-size pieces so that they cook in the same amount of time. Shredding vegetables thinly and slicing them diagonally increases the surface area in contact with the hot oil and speeds up cooking.

Stir-Frying

Success depends on the wok being very hot before you add the oil—hold your hand flat about 2¾ inches/7 cm above the bottom of the wok until you feel the heat. Before you begin, have all the ingredients measured and prepared. Using a long-handled ladle or long, wooden cooking chopsticks, constantly stir the ingredients so that they all come in contact with the hot oil and are evenly cooked.

Deep-Frying

Use enough oil to create a depth of about 2 inches/5 cm. Heat it over a medium–high heat until a faint haze appears. If the oil is not hot enough, the food will act like a sponge and become soggy and greasy. Cook in small batches to avoid overcrowding the pan—too much food will reduce the temperature of the oil and lead to unevenly cooked food. Remove the food with a wire ladle or tongs and drain thoroughly on paper towels.

Steaming

Dependent on fresh ingredients, steaming is routinely used in China to cook a wide range of food, including whole fish, dumplings, vegetables, and morsels of poultry and meat. The food is placed on a plate or in a bamboo steamer above boiling liquid in the bottom of a wok and covered with a lid to trap the steam, which then permeates the food. Depending on size and density, food may be steamed for 10 minutes or up to 3 hours. Ingredients must be fresh to benefit from this technique.

Braising and Red Cooking

Braising is generally used for tougher cuts of meat and vegetables with dense flesh. The ingredients are briefly stir-fried, then simmered in stock until tender. Red cooking is a similar technique in which food is slowly braised in a rich, reddish brown sauce; soy sauce and sugar are key ingredients. Once cooked, the food takes on the color of the sauce and becomes meltingly tender.

Cooking Equipment

Chinese cooking tools and utensils have been used for thousands of years and, as such, have proved their worth. Although Western equivalents do an adequate job, a cleaver and a wok will make life easier when preparing and cooking Chinese food.

Cleaver

Equally useful for demolishing bones or chopping delicate herbs, the rectangular blade of the cleaver is wide, thick, and rigid and tapers down to a razor-sharp edge. It is handy for transferring ingredients from cutting board to wok. Once you become adept, you will be able to use a cleaver to slice, dice, fillet, shred, crush, and chop all kinds of food.

Wok

Traditionally made of iron, the wok conducts heat quickly and evenly—essential in Chinese cooking. During stir-frying, the conical shape tips the food back to the center, where the heat is most intense. If fitted with a lid and a stand for stability, a wok can also be used for steaming, braising, and simmering.

Steamer

The traditional Chinese bamboo steamer has gaps in the bamboo that allow excess moisture to escape, preventing the food from becoming waterlogged. Bamboo steamers come in a range of sizes and can be stacked in a wok or pan of boiling water, letting you cook several dishes at the same time.

Ladle

The Chinese use a special ladle for stir-frying. It has a wide, shallow bowl, which is ideal for lifting, tossing, and turning, and an extra-long handle that lets you keep at a distance from the heat. There are also wire mesh ladles that do an efficient job of scooping up deep-fried foods. The wire lets oil drain away quickly.

Ingredients

Before you start cooking Chinese food, you will need some basic seasonings, oils, and pantry items, many of which you are already likely to have. Most are easily found in supermarkets, health food stores, and Chinese grocers; more obscure items are available by mail order or on-line through the internet. The following basics will get you off to a good start.

ALCOHOLS FOR FLAVORING
Dry sherry or rice wine

NOODLES
Dried egg noodles
Dried rice noodles

NUTS AND SEEDS
Almonds
Cashews
Peanuts
Sesame seeds

OILS
Chili oil and sesame oil for seasoning
Vegetable oil or peanut oil for stir-frying and deep-frying

RICE
White long-grain

SAUCES
Bean sauce, black and yellow
Chili bean sauce
Hoisin sauce
Oyster sauce
Plum sauce
Soy sauce: Use light soy sauce for stir-fries and dark soy sauce for marinades and red cooking

SPICES
Cinnamon sticks
Dried chile flakes
Fennel seeds
Five-spice powder
Ground ginger
Star anise
Sichuan pepper

TOFU (BEAN CURD)
Both firm and soft varieties are useful

VEGETABLES, CANNED OR IN POUCHES
Baby corn
Bamboo shoots
Salted black beans
Straw mushrooms
Water chestnuts

VEGETABLES, DRIED
Dried Chinese mushrooms

VINEGARS
White rice vinegar for rice dishes
Brown rice vinegar for marinades and glazes
Black rice vinegar for slow-cooked stews

Meat and Poultry Dishes

China has countless meat and poultry dishes that are cooked in every imaginable way. Pork is the most widely eaten, with poultry coming a close second. Both are versatile, uniformly tender, and well suited to Chinese cooking methods. There are fewer beef dishes, partly for economic reasons, but also because beef is not as versatile as other meats—only tender cuts are suitable for stir-frying but these dry out during slow-cooking. Ground beef is common in Sichuan cuisine—Ants Climbing a Tree is a classic dish. Lamb is popular in northern China, where religious laws forbid the eating of pork.

Poultry plays an important symbolic role as well as a culinary one. The cock represents positiveness and aggression; the duck, happiness and fidelity; and the pigeon, filial concern and longevity. Turkey sometimes

shows up in Cantonese cooking, but it is not widely eaten in the rest of China because cooks consider it too large to be practical and the flesh can sometimes be dry and tough. In China, poultry is always purchased live, guaranteeing freshness. Obviously, keeping live fowl is not possible—or even desirable—for most Western cooks, but you should buy the best quality you can afford.

Although there are classic meat and poultry dishes throughout China, many of them vary, depending on the region. For example, Beef Chop Suey is a Cantonese classic, but Sichuan cooks spike it with pepper and northerners add plenty of garlic. Sweet-and-Sour Chicken is also typically Cantonese, but Gong Bau Chicken from Sichuan is a complex mix of flavors—hot and spicy as well as sweet and sour.

Wonton Soup

SERVES 6–8

WONTONS

6 oz/175 g ground pork, not too lean

8 oz/225 g shrimp, peeled, deveined, and chopped

½ tsp finely chopped fresh ginger

1 tbsp light soy sauce

1 tbsp Chinese rice wine

2 tsp finely chopped scallion

pinch of sugar

pinch of white pepper

dash of sesame oil

30 square wonton wrappers

1 egg white, lightly beaten

SOUP

8 cups chicken stock

2 tsp salt

½ tsp white pepper

2 tbsp finely chopped scallion

1 tbsp chopped cilantro leaves, to serve

1. For the wonton filling, mix together the pork, shrimp, ginger, soy sauce, rice wine, scallion, sugar, pepper, and sesame oil and stir well until the texture is thick and pasty. Set aside for at least 20 minutes.

2. To make the wontons, place a teaspoon of the filling at the center of a wrapper. Brush the edges with a little egg white. Bring the opposite points toward each other and press the edges together, creating a flowerlike shape. Repeat with the remaining wrappers and filling.

3. To make the soup, bring the stock to a boil and add the salt and pepper. Boil the wontons in the stock for about 5 minutes, or until the wrappers begin to wrinkle around the filling.

4. To serve, put the scallion in individual bowls, then spoon in the wontons and soup and sprinkle with the cilantro.

Ants Climbing a Tree

SERVES 4–6

4 oz/115 g ground pork

4 oz/115 g ground beef

3 tsp light soy sauce

pinch of salt

1 tbsp vegetable or peanut oil

1 tbsp chili bean paste

1 tsp dark soy sauce

¾ cup hot chicken stock

5 oz/140 g thin rice noodles, soaked in warm water for 20 minutes and drained

2 scallions, finely chopped

1. Combine the ground meats with 1 teaspoon of the light soy sauce and the salt.

2. In a preheated wok or deep pan, heat the oil and cook the ground meats until they begin to brown. Add the chili bean paste and stir rapidly. Stir in the dark soy sauce.

3. Pour in the stock, noodles, and remaining light soy sauce. Cover the wok or pan and simmer for about 8–10 minutes, or until the pan is dry. Shake the pan but do not stir. Toss in the scallions and serve.

Hoisin Pork with Garlic Noodles

SERVES 4

9 oz/250 g thick egg noodles or
  whole-wheat egg noodles
1 lb/450 g pork tenderloin, thinly sliced
1 tsp sugar
1 tbsp peanut or corn oil
4 tbsp rice vinegar

4 tbsp white wine vinegar
4 tbsp hoisin sauce
2 scallions, sliced diagonally
about 2 tbsp garlic-flavored oil
2 large garlic cloves, thinly sliced
chopped fresh cilantro, to garnish

1. Cook the noodles in a pan of boiling water for 3 minutes or according to the directions on the package. Drain well, rinse under cold water to stop the cooking, and drain again, then set aside.

2. Meanwhile, sprinkle the pork with the sugar and use your hands to toss together. Heat a wok over high heat. Add the peanut oil and heat until it shimmers. Add the pork and stir-fry for about 3 minutes, until the pork is cooked through and is no longer pink. Use a slotted spoon to remove the pork from the wok and keep warm. Add both vinegars to the wok and boil until they are reduced by about one third. Pour in the hoisin sauce with the scallions and let simmer until reduced by half. Add to the pork and stir together.

3. Quickly wipe out the wok and reheat. Add the garlic-flavored oil and heat until it shimmers. Add the garlic slices and stir around for about 30 seconds, until they are golden and crisp, then use a slotted spoon to scoop them out of the wok and set aside.

4. Add the noodles to the wok and stir them around to warm them through. Divide the noodles among 4 plates, top with the pork-and-scallion mixture, and sprinkle over the garlic slices and cilantro.

Pork Lo Mein

SERVES 4–6

6 oz/175 g boneless lean pork, shredded
8 oz/225 g egg noodles
1½ tbsp vegetable or peanut oil
2 tsp finely chopped garlic
1 tsp finely chopped fresh ginger
1 carrot, julienned
4 cups finely sliced shiitake mushrooms
1 green bell pepper, seeded and thinly sliced
1 tsp salt
½ cup hot chicken stock
1⅓ cups bean sprouts
2 tbsp finely chopped scallion

MARINADE
1 tsp light soy sauce
dash of sesame oil
pinch of white pepper

1. Combine all the marinade ingredients in a bowl and marinate the pork for at least 20 minutes.

2. Cook the noodles in a pan of boiling water for 4–5 minutes, or according to the directions on the package. When cooked, drain and set aside.

3. In a preheated wok or deep pan, heat ½ tablespoon of the oil and stir-fry the pork until the color has changed. Remove and set aside.

4. Quickly wipe out the wok and reheat. Add the remaining oil and stir-fry the garlic and ginger until fragrant. Add the carrot and cook for 1 minute, then add the mushrooms and cook for 1 minute. Toss in the bell pepper and cook for 1 minute. Add the pork, salt, and stock and heat through. Finally, toss in the noodles, followed by the bean sprouts, and stir well. Sprinkle with the scallion and serve.

Fried Rice with Pork and Shrimp

SERVES 4

3 tsp vegetable or peanut oil

1 egg, lightly beaten

3½ oz/100 g shrimp, peeled, deveined, and cut in half

3½ oz/100 g char siu or smoked bacon, finely chopped

2 tbsp finely chopped scallion

3 cups cooked rice, chilled

1 tsp salt

1. In a preheated wok or deep pan, heat 1 teaspoon of the oil and pour in the egg. Cook until scrambled. Remove and set aside.

2. Add the remaining oil and stir-fry the shrimp, cha siu, and scallion for about 2 minutes. Add the rice and salt, breaking up the rice into grains, and cook for an additional 2 minutes. Finally, stir in the cooked egg. Serve immediately.

Sweet-and-Sour Pork

SERVES 4

⅔ cup vegetable oil, for deep-frying

8 oz/225 g pork tenderloin, cut into
   ½-inch/1-cm cubes

1 onion, sliced

1 green bell pepper, seeded and sliced

8 oz/225 g canned pineapple chunks

1 small carrot, cut into thin strips

1 oz/25 g canned bamboo shoots, drained,
   rinsed, and halved

cooked rice, to serve

BATTER

scant ¾ cup all-purpose flour

1 tbsp cornstarch

1½ tsp baking powder

1 tbsp vegetable oil

SAUCE

⅔ cup light brown sugar

2 tbsp cornstarch

½ cup white wine vinegar

2 garlic cloves, crushed

4 tbsp tomato paste

6 tbsp pineapple juice

1. To make the batter, sift the flour into a mixing bowl, together with the cornstarch and baking powder. Add the oil and stir in enough water to make a thick, smooth batter (about ¾ cup).

2. Heat enough oil for deep-frying in a wok, deep-fat fryer, or large, heavy-bottom pan to 350–375°F/180–190°C, or until a cube of bread browns in 30 seconds.

3. Dip the cubes of pork into the batter and cook in the hot oil, in batches, until the pork is cooked through. Remove the pork from the wok with a slotted spoon and drain on paper towels. Set aside and keep the pork pieces warm until they are needed.

4. Drain all but 1 tablespoon of oil from the wok and return it to the heat. Add the onion, bell pepper, pineapple chunks, carrot, and bamboo shoots and cook for 1–2 minutes. Remove from the wok with a slotted spoon and set aside.

5. Mix all of the sauce ingredients together and pour into the wok. Bring to a boil, stirring until thickened and clear. Cook for 1 minute, then return the pork and vegetables to the wok. Cook for an additional 1–2 minutes, then transfer to a serving plate and serve with rice.

Soft-Wrapped Pork and Shrimp Rolls

MAKES 20

4 oz/115 g firm tofu, drained

3 tbsp vegetable or peanut oil

1 tsp finely chopped garlic

2 oz/55 g lean pork, shredded

4 oz/115 g shrimp, peeled and deveined

½ small carrot, cut into short, thin sticks

½ cup fresh or canned bamboo shoots, rinsed
   and shredded (if using fresh shoots, boil in
   water first for 30 minutes)

1 cup finely sliced cabbage

½ cup snow peas, julienned

1-egg omelet, shredded

1 tsp salt

1 tsp light soy sauce

1 tsp Chinese rice wine

pinch of white pepper

20 soft egg roll wrappers

chili bean sauce, to serve

1. Cut the tofu horizontally into thin slices. Heat 1 tablespoon of the oil in a wok and cook the tofu until it turns golden brown. Cut into thin strips and set aside.

2. In a preheated wok or deep pan, heat the remaining oil and stir-fry the garlic until fragrant. Add the pork and stir for about 1 minute, then add the shrimp and stir for an additional minute. One by one, stirring well after each, add the carrot, bamboo shoots, cabbage, snow peas, tofu, and, finally, the shredded omelet. Season with the salt, light soy sauce, rice wine, and pepper. Stir for an additional minute, then turn into a bowl.

3. To assemble each roll, smear an egg roll wrapper with a little chili bean sauce and place a heaped teaspoon of the filling toward the bottom of the circle. Roll up the bottom edge to secure the filling, turn in the sides, and continue to roll up gently. Cut each roll diagonally in half and arrange, cut-sides up, on a serving plate.

Pork and Ginger Dumplings

MAKES 50

1 lb/450 g ground pork, not too lean

1 tbsp light soy sauce

1½ tsp salt

1 tsp Chinese rice wine

½ tsp sesame oil

scant 1 cup very finely chopped cabbage

2 tsp minced fresh ginger

2 tsp finely chopped scallion

½ tsp white pepper

50 round wonton wrappers, about
  2¾ inches/7 cm in diameter

flour, for dusting

peanut oil, for oiling

DIPPING SAUCE

1 tbsp dark soy sauce

1 tbsp rice vinegar

½ tsp sugar

1 tsp chopped fresh ginger

1 tsp chopped garlic

1 fresh Thai red chile, seeded and finely
  chopped

1. To make the dipping sauce, stir all the ingredients together in a small bowl and set aside.

2. For the filling, mix the pork with the light soy sauce and ½ teaspoon of the salt. Stir carefully, always in the same direction, to create a thick paste. Add the rice wine and sesame oil and continue mixing in the same direction. Cover and let rest for at least 20 minutes.

3. To prepare the cabbage, sprinkle the fine shreds with the remaining salt to help draw out the water. Add the ginger, scallion, and white pepper and knead for at least 5 minutes into a thick paste. Combine with the pork mixture.

4. Place about 1 tablespoon of the filling in the center of each wrapper, holding the skin in the palm of one hand. Moisten the edges with water, then seal the edges with 2–3 pleats on each side and place on a lightly floured board.

5. Line a bamboo steamer with a circle of lightly oiled wax paper and replace the lid. Fill the base of the wok with enough water for steaming and place the bamboo steamer on top. Place over medium–high heat and bring to a boil. Transfer the dumplings, in batches, to the steamer, re-cover, and steam for 8–10 minutes, until cooked through. Using a slotted spoon, carefully transfer the dumplings to a serving plate.

6. Pour the dipping sauce into individual bowls, then serve with the dumplings.

Sweet-and-Sour Spareribs

SERVES 4

1 lb/450 g spareribs, cut into bite-size pieces

1½ tbsp vegetable or peanut oil, plus extra for deep-frying

1 green bell pepper, seeded and cut into 1-inch/2.5-cm chunks

1 small onion, coarsely chopped

1 small carrot, finely sliced

½ tsp finely chopped garlic

½ tsp finely chopped fresh ginger

3½ oz/100 g canned pineapple chunks

MARINADE

2 tsp light soy sauce

½ tsp salt

pinch of white pepper

SAUCE

3 tbsp white rice vinegar

2 tbsp sugar

1 tbsp light soy sauce

1 tbsp ketchup

1. Combine the marinade ingredients in a bowl with the spareribs and let marinate for at least 20 minutes.

2. Heat enough oil for deep-frying in a wok, deep-fat fryer, or large, heavy-bottom pan to 350–375°F/ 180–190°C, or until a cube of bread browns in 30 seconds. Deep-fry the spareribs for 8 minutes. Drain and set aside.

3. To make the sauce, mix together the vinegar, sugar, soy sauce, and ketchup. Set aside.

4. In a preheated wok, heat 1 tablespoon of the oil and stir-fry the bell pepper, onion, and carrot for 2 minutes. Remove and set aside.

5. Quickly wipe out the wok and reheat. Add the remaining oil and stir-fry the garlic and ginger until fragrant. Add the sauce, then bring back to a boil and add the pineapple chunks. Finally, add the spareribs and the bell pepper, onion, and carrot. Stir until warmed through and serve immediately.

Pork and Crab Meatballs

SERVES 6

8 oz/225 g pork tenderloin, finely chopped
5¾ oz/170 g canned crabmeat, drained
3 scallions, finely chopped
1 garlic clove, finely chopped
1 tsp Thai red curry paste
1 tbsp cornstarch
1 egg white
vegetable or peanut oil, for deep-frying
cooked rice, to serve

SAUCE
1 tbsp vegetable or peanut oil
2 shallots, chopped
1 garlic clove, crushed
2 large fresh red chiles, seeded and chopped
4 scallions, chopped
3 tomatoes, coarsely chopped

1. Put the pork and crabmeat into a bowl and mix together. Add the scallions, garlic, curry paste, cornstarch, and egg white and beat well to make a thick paste. With damp hands, shape the mixture into walnut-size balls.

2. Heat enough oil for deep-frying in a wok, deep-fat fryer, or large, heavy-bottom pan to 350–375°F/ 180–190°C, or until a cube of bread browns in 30 seconds. Deep-fry the balls, in batches, for 3–4 minutes, turning frequently, until golden brown and cooked. Drain on paper towels and keep warm.

3. To make the sauce, heat the oil in a wok and stir-fry the shallots and garlic for 1–2 minutes. Add the chiles and scallions and stir-fry for 1–2 minutes, then add the tomatoes. Stir together quickly, then spoon the sauce over the pork-and-crab balls. Serve immediately with rice.

Stir-Fried Lamb with Orange

SERVES 4

1 lb/450 g ground lamb

2 garlic cloves, crushed

1 tsp cumin seeds

1 tsp ground coriander

1 red onion, sliced

finely grated rind and juice of 1 orange

2 tbsp light soy sauce

1 orange, peeled and segmented

salt and pepper

snipped fresh chives and strips of orange zest, to garnish

1. Heat a wok or large skillet, without adding any oil. Add the ground lamb to the wok. Dry-fry the ground lamb for 5 minutes, or until the meat is evenly browned. Drain away any excess fat from the wok.

2. Add the garlic, cumin seeds, coriander, and red onion to the wok and cook for an additional 5 minutes.

3. Stir in the orange rind and juice and the soy sauce, mixing until thoroughly combined. Cover, reduce the heat, and let simmer, stirring occasionally, for 15 minutes.

4. Remove the lid, increase the heat, and add the orange segments. Stir to mix.

5. Season with salt and pepper to taste and heat through for an additional 2–3 minutes. Transfer the stir-fry to warmed serving plates and garnish with snipped fresh chives and strips of orange zest. Serve immediately.

Lamb with Black Bean Sauce

SERVES 4

1 lb/450 g lamb neck fillet or boneless
   leg of lamb

1 egg white, lightly beaten

4 tbsp cornstarch

1 tsp Chinese five-spice powder

3 tbsp sunflower oil

1 red onion, sliced

1 red bell pepper, seeded and sliced

1 green bell pepper, seeded and sliced

1 yellow or orange bell pepper,
   seeded and sliced

5 tbsp black bean sauce

cooked noodles, to serve

1. Using a sharp knife, slice the lamb into thin strips.

2. Mix together the egg white, cornstarch, and Chinese five-spice powder. Toss the lamb strips in the mixture until evenly coated.

3. Heat the oil in a wok and cook the lamb over high heat for 5 minutes, or until it crispens around the edges.

4. Add the onion and bell peppers to the wok and cook for 5–6 minutes, or until the vegetables just begin to soften.

5. Stir the black bean sauce into the mixture in the wok and heat through.

6. Transfer to warmed serving dishes and serve hot with noodles.

Beef Chop Suey

SERVES 4

1 lb/450 g rib-eye or sirloin steak, finely sliced

1 head of broccoli, cut into small florets

2 tbsp vegetable or peanut oil

1 onion, finely sliced

2 celery stalks, finely sliced diagonally

2 cups snow peas, sliced in half lengthwise

½ cup fresh or canned bamboo shoots, rinsed and julienned (if using fresh shoots, boil in water first for 30 minutes)

8 water chestnuts, finely sliced

4 cups finely sliced mushrooms

1 tbsp oyster sauce

1 tsp salt

MARINADE

1 tbsp Chinese rice wine

pinch of white pepper

pinch of salt

1 tbsp light soy sauce

½ tsp sesame oil

1. Combine all the marinade ingredients in a bowl and marinate the beef for at least 20 minutes. Blanch the broccoli in a large pan of boiling water for 30 seconds. Drain and set aside.

2. In a preheated wok or deep pan, heat 1 tablespoon of the oil and stir-fry the beef until the color has changed. Remove and set aside.

3. In the clean wok or deep pan, heat the remaining oil and stir-fry the onion for 1 minute. Add the celery and broccoli and cook for 2 minutes. Add the snow peas, bamboo shoots, water chestnuts, and mushrooms and cook for 1 minute. Add the beef, then season with the oyster sauce and salt and serve.

Beef Chow Mein

SERVES 4

10 oz/280 g beef tenderloin, cut into slivers
8 oz/225 g egg noodles
2 tbsp vegetable or peanut oil
1 onion, finely sliced
1 green bell pepper, finely sliced
1 cup bean sprouts
1 tsp salt
pinch of sugar
2 tsp Chinese rice wine
2 tbsp light soy sauce
1 tbsp dark soy sauce
1 tbsp finely shredded scallion

MARINADE
1 tsp light soy sauce
dash of sesame oil
½ tsp Chinese rice wine
pinch of white pepper

1. Combine all the marinade ingredients in a bowl and marinate the beef for at least 20 minutes.

2. Cook the noodles in a pan of boiling water for 4–5 minutes, or according to the directions on the package. When cooked, rinse under cold water and set aside.

3. In a preheated wok or deep pan, heat the oil and stir-fry the beef for about 1 minute, or until it has changed color. Stir in the onion and cook for 1 minute, then add the bell pepper and bean sprouts. Cook until any water from the vegetables has evaporated. Add the salt, sugar, rice wine, and soy sauces. Stir in the noodles and toss for 1 minute. Finally, stir in the scallion and serve.

Sweet-and-Sour Chicken

SERVES 4–6

1 lb/450 g lean chicken, cubed

5 tbsp vegetable or peanut oil

½ tsp minced garlic

½ tsp finely chopped fresh ginger

1 green bell pepper, seeded and cut into
   1-inch/2.5-cm chunks

1 onion, coarsely chopped

1 carrot, finely sliced

1 tsp sesame oil

1 tbsp finely chopped scallion

cooked rice, to serve

MARINADE

2 tsp light soy sauce

1 tsp Chinese rice wine

pinch of white pepper

½ tsp salt

dash of sesame oil

SAUCE

8 tbsp rice vinegar

4 tbsp sugar

2 tsp light soy sauce

6 tbsp ketchup

1. Combine all the marinade ingredients in a bowl and marinate the chicken for at least 20 minutes.

2. To make the sauce, heat the vinegar in a pan and add the sugar, light soy sauce, and ketchup. Stir to dissolve the sugar, then set aside.

3. In a preheated wok, heat 3 tablespoons of the oil and stir-fry the chicken until it starts to turn golden brown. Remove and set aside. Wipe the wok clean.

4. In the clean wok, heat the remaining oil and cook the garlic and ginger until fragrant. Add the vegetables and cook for 2 minutes. Add the chicken and cook for 1 minute. Finally, add the sauce and sesame oil, then stir in the scallion and serve with rice.

Gong Bau Chicken

SERVES 4

2 boneless chicken breasts, with or without skin, cut into ½-inch/1-cm cubes

1 tbsp vegetable or peanut oil

10 dried red chiles or more, to taste, snipped into 2–3 pieces

1 tsp Sichuan peppers

3 garlic cloves, finely sliced

1-inch/2.5-cm piece fresh ginger, finely sliced

1 tbsp coarsely chopped scallion, white part only

generous ½ cup peanuts, roasted

cooked rice, to serve

MARINADE
2 tsp light soy sauce
1 tsp Chinese rice wine
½ tsp sugar

SAUCE
1 tsp light soy sauce
1 tsp dark soy sauce
1 tsp black Chinese rice vinegar
a few drops of sesame oil
2 tbsp chicken stock
1 tsp sugar

1. Combine all the marinade ingredients in a bowl and marinate the chicken, covered, for at least 20 minutes. Combine all the sauce ingredients in a separate bowl and set aside.

2. In a preheated wok, heat the oil and stir-fry the chiles and peppers until crisp and fragrant. Toss in the chicken pieces. When they begin to color, add the garlic, ginger, and scallion. Stir-fry for about 5 minutes, or until the chicken is cooked.

3. Pour in the sauce, mix together thoroughly, then stir in the peanuts. Serve immediately with rice.

Chicken and Shiitake Mushrooms

SERVES 4

2 tbsp vegetable oil

1 lb 8 oz/675 g chicken breast, skinned and cut into 1-inch/2.5-cm chunks

1 tsp grated fresh ginger

3 carrots, thinly sliced

2 onions, thinly sliced

¾ cup bean sprouts

4½ cups fresh or dried shiitake mushrooms, thinly sliced

3 tbsp chopped fresh cilantro

cooked rice noodles, to serve

SAUCE

scant 1 cup granulated sugar

1 cup light soy sauce

1 tsp Chinese five-spice powder

1 cup sweet sherry

1. To make the sauce, combine the sugar, soy sauce, Chinese five-spice powder, and sherry in a bowl. Mix well and set aside.

2. In a wok or skillet, heat the oil over medium–high heat. Add the chicken and stir-fry for 2 minutes, then add the ginger and cook for 1 minute, stirring continuously. Add the sauce and cook for an additional 2 minutes.

3. One at a time, add the carrots, onions, bean sprouts, mushrooms, and cilantro, stirring between each addition.

4. Once the sauce has reduced and is thick, transfer the stir-fry to warmed serving bowls. Serve immediately with noodles.

Cross-the-Bridge Noodles

SERVES 4

10½ oz/300 g thin egg or rice noodles

7 oz/200 g choy sum or similar green vegetable

8 cups chicken stock

½-inch/1-cm piece fresh ginger

1–2 tsp salt

1 tsp sugar

1 boneless, skinless chicken breast, finely sliced diagonally

7 oz/200 g whitefish fillet, finely sliced diagonally

1 tbsp light soy sauce

1. Cook the noodles according to the directions on the package. When cooked, rinse under cold water and set aside. Blanch the choy sum in a large pan of boiling water for 30 seconds. Rinse under cold water and set aside.

2. In a large pan, bring the stock to a boil, then add the ginger, salt, and sugar and skim the surface. Add the chicken and cook for about 4 minutes, then add the fish and simmer for an additional 4 minutes, or until the fish and chicken are cooked through.

3. Add the noodles and choy sum with the light soy sauce and bring back to a boil. Spoon into serving bowls and serve immediately.

Chicken with Cashew Nuts

SERVES 4–6

1 lb/450 g skinless, boneless chicken breast, cut into bite-size pieces

3 tbsp light soy sauce

1 tsp Chinese rice wine

pinch of sugar

½ tsp salt

3 dried Chinese mushrooms, soaked in warm water for 20 minutes

2 tbsp vegetable or peanut oil

4 slices of fresh ginger

1 tsp finely chopped garlic

1 red bell pepper, seeded and cut into 1-inch/2.5-cm chunks

generous ½ cup cashew nuts, roasted

1. Marinate the chicken in 2 tablespoons of the soy sauce, the rice wine, sugar, and salt for at least 20 minutes.

2. Squeeze any excess water from the mushrooms and finely slice, discarding any tough stems. Reserve the soaking water.

3. In a preheated wok, heat 1 tablespoon of the oil. Add the ginger and stir-fry until fragrant. Stir in the chicken and cook for 2 minutes, or until it begins to turn brown. Before the chicken is cooked through, remove and set aside. Wipe the wok clean.

4. In the clean wok, heat the remaining oil and stir-fry the garlic until fragrant. Add the mushrooms and bell pepper and stir-fry for 1 minute. Add about 2 tablespoons of the mushroom soaking water and cook for about 2 minutes, or until the water has evaporated.

5. Return the chicken to the wok, then add the remaining soy sauce and the cashew nuts and stir-fry for 2 minutes, or until the chicken is cooked through. Serve immediately.

Chicken Fried Rice

SERVES 4

½ tbsp sesame oil

6 shallots, peeled and quartered

1 lb/450g cooked chicken, diced

3 tbsp light soy sauce

2 carrots, diced

1 celery stalk, diced

1 red bell pepper, seeded and diced

1½ cups fresh peas

3½ oz/100 g canned corn kernels, drained

4 cups cooked long-grain rice

2 large eggs, scrambled

1. Heat the oil in a large skillet over medium heat. Add the shallots and fry until softened, then add the chicken and 2 tablespoons of the soy sauce and stir-fry for 5–6 minutes.

2. Stir in the carrots, celery, bell pepper, peas, and corn and stir-fry for an additional 5 minutes. Add the rice and stir thoroughly.

3. Finally, stir in the scrambled eggs and the remaining soy sauce. Serve immediately.

Peking Duck

SERVES 6–10

1 duck, about 4 lb 8 oz/2 kg
7 cups boiling water
1 tbsp honey
1 tbsp Chinese rice wine
1 tsp white rice vinegar

TO SERVE
1 cucumber, seeded and julienned
10 scallions, white part only, shredded
30 Peking duck wrappers
plum or hoisin sauce

1. To prepare the duck, massage the skin to separate it from the meat.

2. Pour the boiling water into a large pan, then add the honey, rice wine, and vinegar and lower in the duck. Baste for about 1 minute. Remove the duck and hang it to dry for a few hours or overnight.

3. Preheat the oven to 400°F/200°C. Place the duck on a rack above a roasting pan and roast in the preheated oven for at least 1 hour, or until the skin is crispy and the duck is cooked through.

4. Bring the duck to the table, together with the cucumber, scallions, wrappers, and plum or hoisin sauce. First carve the skin off the duck, then carve the meat. Shred the skin and meat into bite-size strips. Place a little of the duck on a wrapper, top with some cucumber and scallions, and drizzle over a little of the sauce. Roll up the wrapper and repeat with the remaining ingredients. Serve immediately.

Fruity Duck Stir-Fry

SERVES 4

4 duck breasts
1 tsp Chinese five-spice powder
1 tbsp cornstarch
1 tbsp chili oil
8 oz/225 g pearl onions, peeled
2 garlic cloves, crushed

3½ oz/100 g baby corn
1¼ cups canned pineapple chunks, drained
6 scallions, sliced
1 cup bean sprouts
2 tbsp plum sauce

1. Remove any skin from the duck breasts. Cut the duck into thin slices.

2. Mix together the Chinese five-spice powder and cornstarch. Toss the duck in the mixture until well coated.

3. Heat the oil in a preheated wok. Cook the duck for 10 minutes, or until just beginning to crispen around the edges. Remove from the wok and set aside.

4. Add the onions and garlic to the wok and cook for 5 minutes, or until softened. Add the baby corn and cook for an additional 5 minutes. Add the pineapple, scallions, and bean sprouts and cook for 3–4 minutes. Stir in the plum sauce.

5. Return the cooked duck to the wok and toss until well mixed. Transfer to warmed serving dishes and serve hot.

Turkey, Broccoli, and Bok Choy

SERVES 4

1 lb/450 g turkey breast, cut into strips

1 tbsp vegetable oil

1 head of broccoli, cut into florets

2 heads of bok choy, leaves washed and
    separated (or savoy cabbage,
    if bok choy is unavailable)

1 red bell pepper, seeded and thinly sliced

¼ cup chicken stock

MARINADE

1 tbsp light soy sauce

1 tbsp honey

2 garlic cloves, crushed

1. To make the marinade, combine the soy sauce, honey, and garlic in a medium bowl. Add the turkey and toss to coat. Cover the bowl with plastic wrap and let marinate in the refrigerator for 2 hours.

2. Put a wok or large skillet over medium–high heat, add the oil, and heat for 1 minute. Add the turkey and stir-fry for 3 minutes, or until the turkey has changed color. Remove with a slotted spoon, then set aside and keep warm.

3. Add the broccoli, bok choy, and bell pepper to the wok and stir-fry for 2 minutes. Add the stock and continue to stir-fry for 2 minutes, or until the vegetables are crisp yet tender.

4. Return the turkey to the wok and stir-fry briefly to warm through. Serve immediately.

Turkey with Bamboo Shoots and Water Chestnuts

SERVES 4

1 lb/450 g turkey breast, cubed

1 tbsp sesame oil

10 small mushrooms, halved

1 green bell pepper, seeded and cut into strips

1 zucchini, halved and thinly sliced

4 scallions, quartered

4 oz/115 g canned bamboo shoots, drained

4 oz/115 g canned sliced water chestnuts, drained

MARINADE

4 tbsp sweet sherry

1 tbsp lemon juice

1 tbsp light soy sauce

2 tsp grated fresh ginger

1 garlic clove, crushed

1. To make the marinade, combine the sherry, lemon juice, soy sauce, ginger, and garlic in a bowl, then add the turkey and stir. Cover with plastic wrap and let marinate in the refrigerator for 3–4 hours.

2. In a wok or skillet, add the oil and heat. Remove the turkey from the marinade with a slotted spoon (reserving the marinade) and stir-fry a few pieces at a time until browned. Remove the turkey from the wok and set aside.

3. Add the mushrooms, bell pepper, and zucchini to the wok and stir-fry for 3 minutes. Add the scallions and stir-fry for an additional minute. Add the bamboo shoots and water chestnuts to the wok, then add the turkey along with half of the reserved marinade. Stir over medium–high heat for an additional 2–3 minutes, or until the ingredients are evenly coated and the marinade has reduced.

4. Serve immediately in warmed bowls.

Fish and Seafood Dishes

China's extensive coastline and inland waterways offer a huge variety of fresh- and saltwater fish and seafood. Favorites include pike, carp, Mandarin fish (a type of perch), shad, and grouper, plus many other varieties familiar in the West. Shrimp are widely consumed, and scallops, squid, and clams cooked in spicy sauces are also popular.

Somewhat surprisingly, freshwater fish and shellfish play a much bigger part in the Chinese diet than those from the sea, despite 3,000 miles/4,800 km of coastline. This is partly because much of it is farmed in special ponds that are restocked each year, but also because freshwater fish and shellfish, especially crabs and shrimp, are considered sweeter and more delicate than their saltwater equivalents. Soft-shell, freshwater crabs, in particular, are highly prized in Peking.

The Chinese like to cook their fish whole, either steamed, quickly poached, or deep-fried. Lobster and crab are sometimes fried in flavored oil that penetrates the cracked shells, creating a most delectable sauce that the Chinese love to suck from the shells.

Although fish and seafood are commonplace in the kitchen, the Chinese do not like fishy smells. Ginger, garlic, and salty black bean sauce are often used to disguise such smells. Freshness is paramount—no respectable cook would dream of buying anything but a live fish, purchased in a leak-proof basket and kept alive until just before cooking. While this is not usually possible in the West, it is advisable to purchase fish and seafood from a reputable fish supplier. Fresh fish should never smell fishy—this is a sign that it's past its best.

Seafood Chow Mein

SERVES 4

3 oz/85 g squid, cleaned

3–4 prepared scallops

3 oz/85 g shrimp, peeled and deveined

½ egg white, lightly beaten

2 tsp cornstarch, mixed to a paste with 2½ tsp water

9½ oz/275 g egg noodles

5–6 tbsp vegetable oil

2 tbsp light soy sauce

2 oz/55 g snow peas

½ tsp salt

½ tsp sugar

1 tsp Chinese rice wine

2 scallions, finely shredded

a few drops of sesame oil

1. Open up the squid and score the inside in a crisscross pattern, then cut into bite-size pieces. Soak the squid in a bowl of boiling water until all the pieces curl up. Rinse in cold water and drain.

2. Cut each scallop into 3–4 slices. Cut the shrimp in half lengthwise if large. Mix the scallops and shrimp with the egg white and cornstarch paste.

3. Cook the noodles according to the directions on the package. Drain and rinse under cold water. Drain well, then toss with about 1 tablespoon of oil.

4. Heat 3 tablespoons of oil in a preheated wok. Add the noodles and 1 tablespoon of the soy sauce and stir-fry for 2–3 minutes. Transfer to a large serving dish.

5. Heat the remaining oil in the wok and add the snow peas and seafood. Stir-fry for about 2 minutes, then add the salt, sugar, rice wine, the remaining soy sauce, and about half the scallions. Mix well and add a little water if necessary. Pour the seafood mixture on top of the noodles and sprinkle with sesame oil. Garnish with the remaining scallions and serve.

Five-Willow Fish

SERVES 4–6

1 whole sea bass or similar, weighing
  1–1 lb 8 oz/450–675 g, gutted
2 tsp salt
6 tbsp vegetable or peanut oil
2 slices fresh ginger
2 garlic cloves, finely sliced
2 scallions, coarsely chopped
1 green bell pepper, seeded and thinly sliced
1 red bell pepper, seeded and thinly sliced

1 carrot, finely sliced
½ cup fresh or canned bamboo shoots, rinsed
  and thinly sliced (if using fresh shoots, boil in
  water first for 30 minutes)
2 tomatoes, peeled, seeded, and thinly sliced
1 tbsp Chinese rice wine
2 tbsp white rice vinegar
1 tbsp light soy sauce
1 tbsp sugar

1. Clean the fish and dry thoroughly. Score the fish on both sides with deep, diagonal cuts. Press
   ½ teaspoon of the salt into the skin.

2. In a preheated wok, heat 4 tablespoons of the oil and cook the fish for about 4 minutes on each
   side, or until cooked through. Drain, then set aside on a warmed dish and keep warm. Wipe the
   wok clean.

3. In the clean preheated wok, heat the remaining oil and stir-fry the ginger, garlic, and scallions
   until fragrant. Toss in the vegetables with the remaining salt and stir rapidly for 2–3 minutes.
   Add the remaining ingredients and mix well for 2–3 minutes. Pour the sauce over the fish and
   serve immediately.

Salmon and Scallops with Cilantro and Lime

SERVES 4

6 tbsp peanut oil

10 oz/280 g salmon steak, skinned and cut into 1-inch/2.5-cm chunks

8 oz/225 g prepared scallops

3 carrots, thinly sliced

2 celery stalks, cut into 1-inch/2.5-cm pieces

2 yellow bell peppers, seeded and thinly sliced

3 cups oyster mushrooms, thinly sliced

1 garlic clove, crushed

6 tbsp chopped fresh cilantro

3 shallots, thinly sliced

juice of 2 limes

1 tsp grated lime rind

1 tsp dried red pepper flakes

3 tbsp dry sherry

3 tbsp light soy sauce

1. In a large wok or skillet, heat the oil over medium heat. Add the salmon and scallops and stir-fry for 3 minutes. Remove from the wok, then set aside and keep warm.

2. Add the carrots, celery, bell peppers, mushrooms, and garlic to the wok and stir-fry for 3 minutes. Stir in the cilantro and shallots.

3. Add the lime juice and rind, dried red pepper flakes, sherry, and soy sauce and stir. Return the salmon and scallops to the wok and stir-fry carefully for an additional minute. Serve immediately.

Ginger-Marinated Salmon and Scallop Skewers

SERVES 4

RICE SALAD
7 oz/200 g brown basmati rice

½ cucumber, diced

4 scallions, sliced

½ bunch fresh cilantro, chopped

1 red bell pepper, seeded and diced

1 fresh green chile, seeded and thinly sliced

juice of 1 lime

2 tbsp sesame oil

SKEWERS
1 lb 2 oz/500 g salmon fillet, skinned and
  cut into chunks

8 prepared scallops

1½-inch/4-cm piece fresh ginger

juice of 1 lemon

1 tbsp olive oil

salad greens, to serve

1. Bring a large pan of water to a boil, add the rice, and cook for 25 minutes, or until tender. Drain and let cool. Mix the cooled rice with the cucumber, scallions, cilantro, bell pepper, chile, lime juice, and sesame oil in a bowl. Cover and set aside for the flavors to develop.

2. Meanwhile, put the salmon chunks and scallops into a shallow, nonmetallic bowl. Using a garlic press or the back of a knife, crush the ginger to extract the juice. Mix the ginger juice with the lemon juice and olive oil in a small bowl or pitcher and pour over the seafood. Turn the seafood to coat in the marinade. Cover and let marinate in the refrigerator for 30 minutes. Soak 8 wooden skewers in cold water for 30 minutes, then drain.

3. Preheat the broiler to high. Thread the salmon and scallops onto the skewers. Cook under the preheated broiler for 3–4 minutes on each side, or until cooked through.

4. Serve the hot seafood skewers with the rice salad and salad greens.

Monkfish Stir-Fry

SERVES 4

2 tsp sesame oil
1 lb/450 g monkfish fillets, cut into
  1-inch/2.5-cm chunks
1 onion, thinly sliced
3 garlic cloves, finely chopped
1 tsp grated fresh ginger

8 oz/225 g fine asparagus
3 cups thinly sliced mushrooms
2 tbsp light soy sauce
1 tbsp lemon juice

1. Heat the oil in a skillet over medium–high heat. Add the fish, onion, garlic, ginger, asparagus, and mushrooms. Stir-fry for 2–3 minutes.

2. Stir in the soy sauce and lemon juice and cook for an additional minute. Remove from the heat and transfer to warmed serving dishes. Serve immediately.

Fried Fish with Pine Nuts

SERVES 4–6

½ tsp salt

1 lb/450 g thick whitefish fillets, cut into
  1-inch/2.5-cm cubes

2 dried Chinese mushrooms, soaked in warm
  water for 20 minutes

3 tbsp vegetable or peanut oil

1-inch/2.5-cm piece fresh ginger,
  finely shredded

1 tbsp chopped scallion

1 red bell pepper, seeded and cut into
  1-inch/2.5-cm squares

1 green bell pepper, seeded and cut into
  1-inch/2.5-cm squares

¼ cup fresh or canned bamboo shoots, rinsed
  and cut into small cubes (if using fresh
  shoots, boil in water first for 30 minutes)

2 tsp Chinese rice wine

2 tbsp pine nuts, toasted

cooked rice, to serve

1. Sprinkle the salt over the fish and set aside for 20 minutes. Squeeze out any excess water from the mushrooms and finely slice, discarding any tough stems.

2. In a preheated wok, heat 2 tablespoons of the oil and stir-fry the fish for 3 minutes. Drain the fish and set aside, then wipe the wok clean.

3. In the clean, preheated wok, heat the remaining oil and toss in the ginger. Stir until fragrant, then add the scallion, bell peppers, bamboo shoots, mushrooms, and rice wine and cook for 1–2 minutes.

4. Finally, add the fish and stir to warm through. Sprinkle with pine nuts and serve with rice.

Sweet-and-Sour Sea Bass

SERVES 2

scant 1 cup shredded bok choy

generous ¼ cup bean sprouts

generous ½ cup sliced shiitake mushrooms

generous ½ cup torn oyster mushrooms

scant ¼ cup finely sliced scallion

1 tsp finely grated fresh ginger

1 tbsp finely sliced lemongrass

2 skinless, boneless sea bass fillets, about 3¼ oz/90 g each

1 tbsp sesame seeds, toasted

SWEET-AND-SOUR SAUCE

⅓ cup pineapple juice

1 tbsp sugar

1 tbsp red wine vinegar

2 star anise, crushed

⅓ cup tomato juice

1 tbsp cornstarch, blended with a little cold water

1. Preheat the oven to 400°F/200°C. Cut 2 pieces of wax paper into 15-inch/38-cm squares and cut 2 pieces of aluminum foil to the same size.

2. To make the sauce, heat the pineapple juice, sugar, vinegar, star anise, and tomato juice in a pan, let simmer for 1–2 minutes, then thicken with the cornstarch paste, whisking constantly. Pour through a fine strainer into a small bowl and let cool.

3. In a separate large bowl, mix together the bok choy, bean sprouts, mushrooms, and scallion, then add the ginger and lemongrass. Toss all the ingredients together.

4. Put a square of wax paper on top of a square of foil and fold into a triangle. Open up and place half the vegetable mixture into the center, pour half the sauce over the vegetables, and place the sea bass on top. Sprinkle with a few sesame seeds. Close the triangle over the mixture and, starting at the top, fold the right corner and crumple the edges together to form an airtight triangular parcel. Repeat to make the second parcel.

5. Place onto a baking sheet and cook in the preheated oven for 10 minutes, until the foil parcels puff with steam. To serve, place on individual plates and snip the parcels open.

Deep-Fried River Fish with Chili Bean Sauce

SERVES 4–6

1 whole freshwater fish, such as trout or carp, weighing 14 oz/400 g, gutted

1 tbsp all-purpose flour

pinch of salt

scant ½ cup water

vegetable or peanut oil, for deep-frying

SAUCE

scant ½ cup vegetable or peanut oil

1 tsp dried chile flakes

1 garlic clove, finely chopped

1 tsp finely chopped fresh ginger

1 tbsp chili bean sauce

½ tsp white pepper

2 tsp sugar

1 tbsp white rice vinegar

1 tsp finely chopped scallion

1. To prepare the fish, clean and dry thoroughly. Mix together the flour, salt, and water to create a light batter. Use to coat the fish.

2. Heat enough oil for deep-frying in a wok, deep-fat fryer, or large, heavy-bottom pan to 350–375°F/ 180–190°C, or until a cube of bread browns in 30 seconds. Deep-fry the fish on one side at a time until the skin is crisp and golden brown. Drain, then set aside and keep warm.

3. To make the sauce, first heat all but 1 tablespoon of the oil in a small pan and, when smoking, pour over the chile flakes. Set aside.

4. In a preheated wok or deep pan, heat the remaining oil and stir-fry the garlic and ginger until fragrant. Stir in the chili bean sauce, then add the oil-and-chile flake mixture. Season with the pepper, sugar, and vinegar. Turn off the heat and stir in the scallion. Pour over the fish and serve immediately.

Wok-Fried Jumbo Shrimp in Spicy Sauce

SERVES 4

3 tbsp vegetable or peanut oil

1 lb/450 g jumbo shrimp, deveined but unpeeled

2 tsp finely chopped fresh ginger

1 tsp finely chopped garlic

1 tbsp chopped scallion

2 tbsp chili bean sauce

1 tsp Chinese rice wine

1 tsp sugar

½ tsp light soy sauce

1–2 tbsp chicken stock

1. In a preheated wok, heat the oil, then add in the shrimp and stir-fry over high heat for about 4 minutes. Arrange the shrimp on the sides of the wok out of the oil, then add in the ginger and garlic and stir until fragrant. Add the scallion and chili bean sauce. Stir the shrimp into this mixture.

2. Reduce the heat slightly and add the rice wine, sugar, soy sauce, and stock. Cover and cook for an additional minute. Serve immediately.

Ginger Shrimp with Oyster Mushrooms

SERVES 4

SAUCE
⅔ cup chicken stock
2 tsp sesame seeds
3 tsp grated fresh ginger
1 tbsp light soy sauce
¼ tsp hot pepper sauce
1 tsp cornstarch

3–4 tbsp vegetable oil
3 carrots, thinly sliced
7 cups thinly sliced oyster mushrooms
1 large red bell pepper, seeded and
    thinly sliced
1 lb/450 g large shrimp, peeled and deveined
2 garlic cloves, crushed
fresh cilantro leaves, to garnish
cooked rice, to serve

1. To make the sauce, stir together the stock, sesame seeds, ginger, soy sauce, hot pepper sauce, and cornstarch in a small bowl until well blended. Set aside.

2. In a large wok or skillet, heat 2 tablespoons of the oil. Stir-fry the carrots for 3 minutes, then remove from the wok and set aside.

3. Add 1 tablespoon of the remaining oil to the wok and cook the mushrooms for 2 minutes. Remove from the wok and set aside.

4. Add the remaining oil to the wok, if needed, and stir-fry the bell pepper with the shrimp and garlic for 3 minutes, or until the shrimp turn pink and opaque.

5. Stir the sauce and pour it into the wok. Cook until the mixture bubbles, then return the carrots and mushrooms to the wok. Cover and cook for an additional 2 minutes, or until heated through.

6. Garnish with cilantro leaves and serve immediately with rice.

Shrimp Fu Yung

SERVES 4–6

1 tbsp vegetable or peanut oil
4 oz/115 g large shrimp, peeled and deveined
4 eggs, lightly beaten

1 tsp salt
pinch of white pepper
2 tbsp snipped Chinese chives

1. In a preheated wok, heat the oil and stir-fry the shrimp until they begin to turn pink.

2. Season the eggs with the salt and pepper and pour over the shrimp. Stir-fry for 1 minute, then add the chives.

3. Cook for an additional 4 minutes, stirring all the time, until the eggs are cooked through but still soft in texture. Serve immediately.

Drunken Shrimp

SERVES 4–6

7 oz/200 g jumbo shrimp, peeled and deveined
1¼ cups Chinese rice wine
2 tbsp cognac

½ tsp salt
1 tbsp finely chopped scallion
1 tsp finely chopped fresh ginger

1. Blanch the shrimp in a large pan of boiling water for 30 seconds. Drain and set aside.

2. Combine all the ingredients, then cover and let stand at room temperature for about 1 hour. Strain and serve cold.

Chiles Stuffed with Fish Paste

SERVES 4–6

8 oz/225 g whitefish, ground

2 tbsp lightly beaten egg

4–6 large fresh red and green chiles

1 tbsp vegetable or peanut oil, plus extra for shallow-frying

2 garlic cloves, finely chopped

½ tsp fermented black beans, rinsed and lightly mashed

1 tbsp light soy sauce

pinch of sugar

1 tbsp water

MARINADE

1 tsp finely chopped fresh ginger

pinch of salt

pinch of white pepper

½ tsp vegetable or peanut oil

1. To make the marinade, combine all the ingredients in a bowl and marinate the fish for 20 minutes. Add the egg and mix by hand to create a smooth fish paste.

2. To prepare the chiles, cut in half lengthwise and scoop out the seeds and membranes. Cut into bite-size pieces. Spread each piece of chile with about ½ teaspoon of the fish paste.

3. In a preheated wok, heat enough oil for shallow-frying and cook the chile pieces on both sides, until they begin to turn golden brown. Drain the chiles, set aside, and wipe the wok clean.

4. Heat the 1 tablespoon of oil in the clean wok and stir-fry the garlic until aromatic. Stir in the black beans and mix well. Add the soy sauce and sugar and stir, then add the chile pieces. Add the water, then cover and simmer over a low heat for 5 minutes. Serve immediately.

Crispy Crab Wontons

MAKES 24

6 oz/175 g white crabmeat, drained if canned
   and thawed if frozen, flaked
1¾ oz/50 g canned water chestnuts, drained,
   rinsed, and chopped
1 small fresh red chile, chopped
1 scallion, chopped
1 tbsp cornstarch

1 tsp dry sherry
1 tsp light soy sauce
½ tsp lime juice
24 square wonton wrappers
vegetable oil, for deep-frying
fresh chives and lime slices, to garnish

1. To make the filling, mix the crabmeat, water chestnuts, chile, scallion, cornstarch, sherry, soy sauce, and lime juice together in a bowl.

2. Spread the wonton wrappers out on a counter and spoon an equal portion of the filling into the center of each wonton wrapper.

3. Dampen the edges of the wonton wrappers with a little water and fold them in half to form triangles. Fold the 2 bottom corners in toward the center, moisten with a little water to secure, then pinch together to seal.

4. Heat enough oil for deep-frying in a wok, deep-fat fryer, or large, heavy-bottom pan to 350–375°F/ 180–190°C, or until a cube of bread browns in 30 seconds. Deep-fry the wontons in batches for 2–3 minutes, until golden brown and crisp. Remove with a slotted spoon and drain on paper towels.

5. Serve the wontons hot, garnished with chives and lime slices.

Scallops in Black Bean Sauce

SERVES 4

2 tbsp vegetable or peanut oil

1 tsp finely chopped garlic

1 tsp finely chopped fresh ginger

1 tbsp fermented black beans, rinsed and
lightly mashed

14 oz/400 g prepared scallops

½ tsp light soy sauce

1 tsp Chinese rice wine

1 tsp sugar

3–4 fresh red Thai chiles, finely chopped

1–2 tsp chicken stock

1 tbsp finely chopped scallion

1. Heat the oil in a preheated wok. Add the garlic and stir, then add the ginger and stir-fry together for about 1 minute, or until fragrant. Mix in the black beans, add the scallops, and stir-fry for 1 minute. Add the soy sauce, rice wine, sugar, and chiles.

2. Reduce the heat and simmer for 2 minutes, then add the stock. Finally, add the scallion, then stir and serve.

Baby Squid Stuffed with Pork and Mushrooms

SERVES 6–8

14 oz/400 g squid
4 dried Chinese mushrooms, soaked in warm
  water for 20 minutes
8 oz/225 g ground pork
4 water chestnuts, finely chopped
½ tsp sesame oil
1 tsp salt
½ tsp white pepper
vegetable oil, for oiling

DIPPING SAUCE
4 tbsp dark soy sauce
1 fresh red Thai chile, chopped (optional)

1. Clean the squid thoroughly, removing all the tentacles. Squeeze out any excess water from the mushrooms and finely chop, discarding any tough stems.

2. Mix the mushrooms with the pork, water chestnuts, oil, salt, and pepper.

3. Force the stuffing into the squids, pressing firmly but leaving enough room to secure each one with a toothpick.

4. Line a bamboo steamer with a circle of lightly oiled wax paper and replace the lid. Fill the bottom of a wok with enough water for steaming and place the bamboo steamer on top. Place over medium–high heat and bring to a boil. Transfer the squid to the steamer, re-cover, and steam for 15 minutes, until cooked through.

5. Meanwhile, make the dipping sauce. Pour the soy sauce into a small serving bowl and mix in the chile, if using. Set aside.

6. Using a slotted spoon, carefully transfer the squid to a serving plate. Serve with the dipping sauce.

Stir-Fried Squid with Hot Black Bean Sauce

SERVES 4

1 lb 10 oz/750 g squid, cleaned and
   tentacles discarded
1 large red bell pepper, seeded
scant 1 cup snow peas
1 head of bok choy
1 tbsp corn oil
1 small fresh red Thai chile, chopped
1 garlic clove, finely chopped
1 tsp grated fresh ginger
2 scallions, chopped

SAUCE
3 tbsp black bean sauce
1 tbsp Thai fish sauce
1 tbsp rice wine or dry sherry
1 tbsp dark soy sauce
1 tsp brown sugar
1 tsp cornstarch
1 tbsp water

1. Cut the squid body cavities into quarters lengthwise. Use the tip of a small, sharp knife to score a diamond pattern into the flesh without cutting all the way through. Pat dry with paper towels.

2. Cut the bell pepper into long, thin slices. Cut the snow peas in half diagonally. Coarsely shred the bok choy.

3. To make the sauce, mix the black bean sauce, fish sauce, rice wine, soy sauce, and sugar together in a bowl. Blend the cornstarch with the water and stir into the other ingredients in the bowl. Reserve the mixture until required.

4. Heat the oil in a preheated wok. Add the chile, garlic, ginger, and scallions and stir-fry for 1 minute. Add the bell pepper slices and stir-fry for 2 minutes.

5. Add the squid and stir-fry over high heat for an additional minute. Stir in the snow peas and bok choy and stir for an additional minute, or until the bok choy has wilted.

6. Stir in the sauce ingredients and cook, stirring constantly, for 2 minutes, or until the sauce thickens and clears. Serve immediately on warmed plates.

Sweet Chile Squid

SERVES 4

2½ tbsp sesame oil
10 oz/280 g prepared squid, cut into strips
2 red bell peppers, seeded and thinly sliced
3 shallots, thinly sliced
1½ cups mushrooms, thinly sliced
1 tbsp dry sherry
4 tbsp light soy sauce

1 tsp sugar
1 tsp hot chile flakes, or to taste
1 garlic clove, crushed
1 tbsp sesame seeds, toasted
cooked rice, to serve

1. Heat 1 tablespoon of the oil in a skillet over medium heat. Add the squid and cook for 2 minutes. Remove from the skillet and set aside.

2. Add 1 tablespoon of the remaining oil to the skillet and cook the bell peppers and shallots over medium heat for 1 minute. Add the mushrooms and cook for an additional 2 minutes.

3. Return the squid to the skillet and add the sherry, soy sauce, sugar, chile flakes, and garlic, stirring thoroughly. Cook for another 2 minutes.

4. Sprinkle with the sesame seeds, then drizzle over the remaining oil and mix. Serve immediately with rice.

Stir-Fried Fresh Crab with Ginger

SERVES 4

3 tbsp vegetable or peanut oil

2 large fresh crabs, cleaned, broken into pieces, and legs cracked with a cleaver

1½-inch/4-cm piece fresh ginger, julienned

7 scallions, chopped into 2-inch/5-cm lengths

2 tbsp light soy sauce

1 tsp sugar

pinch of white pepper

1. In a preheated wok, heat 2 tablespoons of the oil and cook the crab over high heat for 3–4 minutes. Remove and set aside. Wipe the wok clean.

2. In the clean wok, heat the remaining oil, then add the ginger and stir until fragrant. Add the scallions, then stir in the crab pieces. Add the soy sauce, sugar, and pepper. Cover and simmer for 1 minute, then serve immediately in warmed bowls.

Clams in Black Bean Sauce

SERVES 4

2 lb/900 g small clams

1 tbsp vegetable or peanut oil

1 tsp finely chopped fresh ginger

1 tsp finely chopped garlic

1 tbsp fermented black beans, rinsed and
coarsely chopped

2 tsp Chinese rice wine

1 tbsp finely chopped scallion

1 tsp salt (optional)

1. Discard any clams with broken shells and any that refuse to close when tapped. Wash the remaining clams thoroughly and let soak in clean water until ready to cook.

2. In a preheated wok, heat the oil and stir-fry the ginger and garlic until fragrant. Add the black beans and cook for 1 minute.

3. Over a high heat, add the clams and rice wine and stir-fry for 2 minutes to mix everything together. Cover and cook for about 3 minutes. Discard any clams that remain closed. Add the scallion and salt, if needed, and serve immediately.

Vegetable Dishes

Because of its vast size and varying climate, China produces an amazing variety of vegetables and the Chinese have perfected the art of cooking them. Cooks visit the market on a daily basis to make sure they get the freshest and best vegetables available; anything even slightly substandard will be firmly rejected.

Vegetables are integral to every meal and far more are consumed than meat or poultry. With few exceptions, meat and poultry dishes are always combined with some kind of vegetable, and soups often include slivers of colorful vegetables, such as bell peppers, boy choy, and carrots, and tasty flavorings, such as ginger and chiles. Stir-frying, in which ingredients are quickly cooked over high heat, is the usual way of cooking vegetables. The technique ensures that all-important flavor, color, and texture, as well as valuable nutrients, are preserved.

Salads as we know them in the West do not feature greatly on the Chinese menu, except perhaps in the Canton region, where chefs are more inclined to try out new ideas from abroad. However, many lightly cooked vegetable dishes can be classified as salads if they are cooled and lightly tossed in a dressing.

Tofu (bean curd) made from soybeans is eaten throughout China but is particularly popular in the north, where soybeans are an important crop. Hot-and-Sour Soup with Tofu, and Mushroom and Tofu Firepot are typical of hearty Mongolian cuisine. In regions where wheat is the staple, you'll find vegetable and noodle combinations instead of rice. Try Sweet-and-Sour Vegetables on Noodle Pancakes, or Chengdu Noodles in Sesame Sauce—a spicy Sichuan dish that is traditionally eaten cold.

Hot-and-Sour Soup with Tofu

SERVES 4

3 strips of lime zest

2 garlic cloves, peeled

2 slices fresh ginger

4 cups chicken stock

1 tbsp vegetable oil

6 oz/175 g firm tofu, drained and cubed

7 oz/200 g fine egg noodles

1½ cups sliced shiitake mushrooms

1 fresh red chile, seeded and sliced

4 scallions, sliced

1 tsp light soy sauce

juice of 1 lime

1 tsp Chinese rice wine

1 tsp sesame oil

chopped fresh cilantro, to garnish

1. Put the lime zest, garlic, and ginger into a large pan with the stock and bring to a boil. Reduce the heat and let simmer for 5 minutes. Remove the lime zest, garlic, and ginger with a slotted spoon and discard.

2. Meanwhile, heat the vegetable oil in a large skillet over high heat, add the tofu, and cook, turning frequently, until golden. Remove the tofu from the skillet and drain on paper towels.

3. Add the noodles, mushrooms, and chile to the stock and let simmer for 3 minutes.

4. Add the tofu, scallions, soy sauce, lime juice, rice wine, and sesame oil and briefly heat through.

5. Divide the soup among 4 warmed bowls, sprinkle over the cilantro, and serve immediately.

Mushroom and Ginger Soup

SERVES 4

½ oz/15 g dried Chinese mushrooms or
    4½ oz/125 g portobello or cremini
    mushrooms
4 cups hot vegetable stock
4½ oz/125 g thin egg noodles
2 tsp corn oil

3 garlic cloves, crushed
1-inch/2.5-cm piece fresh ginger,
    finely shredded
1 tsp light soy sauce
1¼ cups bean sprouts
fresh cilantro leaves, to garnish

1. Soak the dried Chinese mushrooms for at least 30 minutes in 1¼ cups of the hot stock. Drain the mushrooms and reserve the stock. Remove the stems of the mushrooms and discard. Slice the caps and reserve.

2. Cook the noodles according to the directions on the package. Drain well, rinse under cold water, and drain again. Set aside.

3. Heat the oil in a preheated wok or large, heavy-bottom skillet over high heat. Add the garlic and ginger, stir, and add the mushrooms. Stir over high heat for 2 minutes.

4. Add the remaining stock with the reserved mushroom soaking liquid and bring to a boil. Add the soy sauce. Stir in the bean sprouts and cook until tender.

5. Divide the noodles among 4 serving bowls and ladle the soup on top. Garnish with cilantro leaves and serve immediately.

Classic Stir-Fried Vegetables

SERVES 4

3 tbsp sesame oil

8 scallions, chopped

1 garlic clove, crushed

1 tbsp grated fresh ginger

1 head of broccoli, cut into florets

1 yellow or orange bell pepper, seeded and coarsely chopped

1 cup shredded red cabbage

4½ oz/125 g baby corn

2 cups thinly sliced portobello mushrooms

1⅓ cups fresh bean sprouts

9 oz/250 g canned water chestnuts, drained

4 tsp light soy sauce

1. Heat 2 tablespoons of the oil in a large skillet or wok over high heat. Stir-fry two thirds of the scallions with the garlic and ginger for 30 seconds.

2. Add the broccoli, bell pepper, and red cabbage and stir-fry for 1–2 minutes. Mix in the baby corn and mushrooms and stir-fry for an additional 1–2 minutes.

3. Finally, add the bean sprouts and water chestnuts and cook for an additional 2 minutes. Pour in the soy sauce and stir well.

4. Transfer to warmed dishes and serve immediately, garnished with the remaining scallions.

Bamboo Shoots with Tofu

SERVES 4–6

3 dried Chinese mushrooms, soaked in warm water for 20 minutes

1 cup baby bok choy (if unavailable use 1 head regular bok choy, thickly sliced)

1 lb/450 g firm tofu, drained and cut into 1-inch/2.5-cm squares

1 tbsp vegetable or peanut oil, plus extra for deep-frying

½ cup fresh or canned bamboo shoots, rinsed and finely sliced (if using fresh shoots, boil in water first for 30 minutes)

1 tsp oyster sauce

1 tsp light soy sauce

1. Squeeze out any excess water from the mushrooms and finely slice, discarding any tough stems.

2. Blanch the bok choy in a large pan of boiling water for 30 seconds. Drain and set aside.

3. Heat enough oil for deep-frying in a wok, deep-fat fryer, or large, heavy-bottom pan to 350–375°F/ 180–190°C, or until a cube of bread browns in 30 seconds. Fry the tofu until golden brown. Remove, drain on paper towels, and set aside.

4. In a preheated wok or deep pan, heat the 1 tablespoon of oil, toss in the mushrooms and bok choy, and stir. Add the tofu and bamboo shoots with the oyster sauce and soy sauce. Heat through and serve.

Spicy Tofu

SERVES 4

9 oz/250 g firm tofu, rinsed, drained, and cut
    into ½-inch/1-cm cubes
4 tbsp peanut oil
1 tbsp grated fresh ginger
3 garlic cloves, crushed
4 scallions, thinly sliced
1 head of broccoli, cut into florets
1 carrot, cut into batons
1 yellow bell pepper, seeded and thinly sliced
2¾ cups thinly sliced shiitake mushrooms
cooked rice, to serve

MARINADE
5 tbsp vegetable stock
2 tsp cornstarch
2 tbsp light soy sauce
1 tbsp superfine sugar
pinch of chile flakes

1. To make the marinade, mix the stock, cornstarch, soy sauce, sugar, and chile flakes together in a large bowl. Add the tofu and toss well to cover in the marinade. Set aside to marinate for 20 minutes.

2. In a large skillet or wok, heat 2 tablespoons of the oil and stir-fry the tofu with its marinade until brown and crispy. Remove from the skillet and set aside.

3. Heat the remaining oil in the skillet and stir-fry the ginger, garlic, and scallions for 30 seconds. Add the broccoli, carrot, bell pepper, and mushrooms and cook for 5–6 minutes. Return the tofu to the skillet and stir-fry to heat through. Serve immediately with rice.

Mixed Vegetables with Quick-Fried Basil

SERVES 4

2 tbsp vegetable or peanut oil, plus extra for shallow-frying

2 garlic cloves, chopped

1 onion, sliced

4 oz/115 g baby corn, cut in half diagonally

½ cucumber, peeled, halved, seeded, and sliced

8 oz/225 g canned water chestnuts, drained and rinsed

¾ cup snow peas

2 cups shiitake mushrooms, halved

1 red bell pepper, seeded and thinly sliced

1 tbsp light brown sugar

2 tbsp light soy sauce

1 tbsp fish sauce

1 tbsp rice vinegar

8–12 sprigs fresh Thai basil

cooked rice, to serve

1. Heat the oil in a wok and stir-fry the garlic and onion for 1–2 minutes. Add the baby corn, cucumber, water chestnuts, snow peas, mushrooms, and bell pepper and stir-fry for 2–3 minutes, until starting to soften.

2. Add the sugar, soy sauce, fish sauce, and vinegar and gradually bring to a boil. Let simmer for 1–2 minutes.

3. Meanwhile, heat enough oil for shallow-frying in a wok. When hot, add the basil sprigs and cook for 20–30 seconds, until crisp. Remove with a slotted spoon and drain on paper towels.

4. Garnish the vegetable stir-fry with the crispy basil and serve immediately with rice.

Oyster Mushrooms and Vegetables with Peanut Chili Sauce

SERVES 4

1 tbsp vegetable or peanut oil

4 scallions, finely sliced

1 carrot, cut into thin strips

1 zucchini, cut into thin strips

½ head of broccoli, cut into florets

9 cups oyster mushrooms, thinly sliced

2 tbsp crunchy peanut butter

1 tsp chili powder, or to taste

3 tbsp water

cooked rice, to serve

lime wedges, to garnish

1. Heat the oil in a wok until almost smoking. Stir-fry the scallions for 1 minute. Add the carrot and zucchini and stir-fry for 1 minute, then add the broccoli and cook for an additional minute.

2. Stir in the mushrooms and cook until they have softened and at least half the liquid they produce has evaporated. Add the peanut butter and stir well. Season with the chili powder to taste. Finally, add the water and cook for an additional minute.

3. Serve with rice and garnish with lime wedges.

Broccoli and Snow Pea Stir-Fry

SERVES 4

2 tbsp vegetable or peanut oil

dash of sesame oil

1 garlic clove, finely chopped

1½ cups small broccoli florets

1 cup snow peas

3 cups thickly sliced Chinese cabbage

5–6 scallions, finely chopped

½ tsp salt

2 tbsp light soy sauce

1 tbsp Chinese rice wine

1 tsp sesame seeds, lightly toasted

1. In a preheated wok, heat the oils, then add the garlic and stir-fry vigorously. Add all the vegetables and salt and stir-fry over high heat, tossing rapidly, for about 3 minutes.

2. Pour in the soy sauce and rice wine and cook for an additional 2 minutes. Sprinkle with the sesame seeds and serve hot.

Choy Sum in Oyster Sauce

SERVES 4–6

10½ oz/300 g choy sum
1 tbsp vegetable or peanut oil

1 tsp finely chopped garlic
1 tbsp oyster sauce

1. Blanch the choy sum in a large pan of boiling water for 30 seconds. Drain and set aside.

2. In a preheated wok or deep pan, heat the oil and stir-fry the garlic until fragrant. Add the choy sum and toss for 1 minute. Stir in the oyster sauce and serve.

Eggplants With Red Bell Pepper

SERVES 4

3 tbsp vegetable or peanut oil

1 garlic clove, finely chopped

3 eggplants, halved lengthwise and cut diagonally into 1-inch/2.5-cm pieces

1 tsp white rice vinegar

1 red bell pepper, seeded and finely sliced

2 tbsp light soy sauce

1 tsp sugar

1 tbsp finely chopped cilantro leaves (optional), to garnish

1. In a preheated wok or deep pan, heat the oil. When it begins to smoke, toss in the garlic and stir-fry until fragrant, then add the eggplants. Stir-fry for 30 seconds, then add the vinegar. Turn down the heat and cook, covered, for 5 minutes, stirring from time to time.

2. When the eggplant pieces are soft, add the bell pepper and stir. Add the soy sauce and sugar and cook, uncovered, for 2 minutes.

3. Turn off the heat and let rest for 2 minutes. Transfer to a dish, then garnish with cilantro and serve.

Stuffed Eggplant with Spicy Sauce

SERVES 5–6

BATTER
⅔ cup chickpea flour

⅓ cup all-purpose flour

pinch of salt

1 egg, beaten

1¼ cups very cold water

STUFFING
3½ oz/100 g ground pork

½ tsp finely chopped scallion

½ tsp finely chopped fresh ginger

dash of Chinese rice wine

pinch of white pepper

pinch of salt

SPICY SAUCE
2-inch/5-cm piece fresh ginger

2 large garlic cloves

2 tbsp vegetable or peanut oil

3 tbsp chili bean sauce

1 tsp white rice vinegar

2 tsp sugar

⅔ cup chicken stock

2 large eggplants, cut into
   1½ inch/4 cm thick slices

vegetable or peanut oil, for deep-frying

1. To prepare the batter, sift together the flours and salt into a large bowl. Stir in the egg, then gradually add the water. Beat for at least 5 minutes, or until the batter is smooth and thick. Let rest in the refrigerator.

2. To prepare the stuffing, mix together all the ingredients and let stand for 20 minutes.

3. Make a small incision—cut less than halfway through—on the side of each eggplant slice. Stuff about ½ teaspoon of the pork stuffing into the incision, smoothing the surface with a knife to remove any excess.

4. Heat enough oil for deep-frying in a wok, deep-fat fryer, or large, heavy-bottom pan to 350–375°F/ 180–190°C, or until a cube of bread browns in 30 seconds. Dip each eggplant slice into the batter and lower straight into the oil. Cook for about 10 minutes, or until golden brown. Drain on paper towels and arrange in a bowl or on a serving plate.

5. Grate the ginger and garlic for the sauce on a very fine grater, discarding the fibrous parts left on top of the grater and reserving the juices.

6. Heat the oil in a preheated wok or deep pan. Add the chili bean sauce and stir for 1 minute, then reduce the heat. Add the ginger and garlic juice and stir-fry for 1 minute, then add the vinegar and sugar and cook for 2 minutes. Finally, add the stock and simmer for 2 minutes. Serve the stuffed eggplant slices with the sauce.

Sweet-and-Sour Vegetables on Noodle Pancakes

SERVES 4

4 oz/115 g thin rice noodles
2 lb/900 g selection of vegetables, such as carrots, baby corn, mushrooms, broccoli, snow peas, and onions
6 eggs
4 scallions, sliced diagonally

2½ tbsp peanut or corn oil
3½ oz/100 g canned bamboo shoots, drained
scant 1 cup store-bought sweet-and-sour sauce
salt and pepper

1. Soak the noodles in enough lukewarm water to cover and let stand for 20 minutes, until softened. Alternatively, cook according to the directions on the package. Drain well and use scissors to cut into 3-inch/7.5-cm pieces, then set aside.

2. Meanwhile, prepare the vegetables as necessary and chop into equal-size chunks.

3. Beat the eggs in a large bowl, then stir in the noodles and scallions and season to taste with salt and pepper. Heat an 8-inch/20-cm skillet over high heat. Add 1 tablespoon of the oil and swirl it around. Pour in one quarter of the egg mixture and tilt the skillet so it covers the bottom. Reduce the heat to medium and cook for 1 minute, or until the thin pancake is set. Flip it over and continue cooking until the pancake is set. Keep warm in a low oven while you make 3 more pancakes.

4. Heat a wok or large skillet over high heat. Add the remaining oil and heat until it shimmers. Add the thickest vegetables, such as carrots, first and stir-fry for 30 seconds. Gradually add the remaining vegetables and the bamboo shoots. Stir in the sauce and stir-fry until all the vegetables are tender and the sauce is hot. Spoon the vegetables and sauce over the pancakes and serve.

Sweet-and-Sour Vegetables with Cashew Nuts

SERVES 4

1 tbsp vegetable or peanut oil

1 tsp chili oil

2 onions, sliced

2 carrots, thinly sliced

2 zucchini, thinly sliced

1 small head of broccoli, cut into small florets

2¼ cups sliced mushrooms

2 heads of baby bok choy, sliced

2 tbsp light brown sugar

2 tbsp light soy sauce

1 tbsp rice vinegar

scant ½ cup cashew nuts

1. Heat the oils in a wok and stir-fry the onions for 1–2 minutes, until they start to soften.

2. Add the carrots, zucchini, and broccoli and stir-fry for 2–3 minutes. Add the mushrooms, bok choy, sugar, soy sauce, and vinegar and stir-fry for 1–2 minutes.

3. Meanwhile, dry-fry the cashew nuts in a small skillet until lightly colored. Sprinkle the cashew nuts over the stir-fry and serve immediately.

Mushroom and Tofu Firepot

SERVES 4

2 oz/55 g dried Chinese mushrooms

4 oz/115 g firm tofu, drained

2 tbsp sweet chili sauce

2 tbsp peanut or corn oil

2 large garlic cloves, chopped

½-inch/1-cm piece fresh ginger, finely chopped

1 red onion, sliced

½ tbsp Sichuan peppers, lightly crushed

4 oz/115 g canned straw mushrooms, drained and rinsed

1 star anise

pinch of sugar

soy sauce, to taste

4 oz/115 g thin rice noodles

1. Soak the mushrooms in enough boiling water to cover for 20 minutes, or until softened. Cut the tofu into bite-size chunks and stir with the sweet chili sauce until coated, then let marinate.

2. Strain the soaked mushrooms through a strainer lined with a paper towel, reserving the soaking liquid. Heat the oil in a medium flameproof casserole or large skillet with a lid. Add the garlic and ginger and stir them around for 30 seconds. Add the onion and peppers and keep stirring until the onion is almost tender. Add the tofu, the soaked mushrooms, and the straw mushrooms and stir around carefully so the tofu doesn't break up.

3. Add the reserved strained mushroom soaking liquid to the wok with just enough water to cover the tofu mixture. Stir in the star anise and sugar with several dashes of soy sauce, or to taste. Bring to a boil, then reduce the heat to the lowest setting, cover, and let simmer for 5 minutes. Add the noodles to the wok, re-cover, and simmer for an additional 5 minutes, or until the noodles are tender. The noodles should be covered with liquid, so add extra water at this point, if necessary. Use a fork or wooden spoon to stir the noodles into the other ingredients. Serve immediately.

Braised Straw Mushrooms

SERVES 4

1 tbsp vegetable or peanut oil

1 tsp finely chopped garlic

6 oz/175 g straw mushrooms,
  washed but left whole

2 tsp fermented black beans,
  rinsed and lightly mashed

1 tsp sugar

1 tbsp light soy sauce

1 tsp dark soy sauce

1. Heat the oil in a small flameproof casserole. Cook the garlic until fragrant, then add the mushrooms and stir well to coat in the oil.

2. Add the beans, sugar, and soy sauces, then reduce the heat and simmer, covered, for about 10 minutes, or until the mushrooms have softened. Serve immediately.

Vegetable and Coconut Curry

SERVES 4

1 onion, coarsely chopped

3 garlic cloves, thinly sliced

1-inch/2.5-cm piece fresh ginger,
   thinly sliced

2 fresh green chiles, seeded and
   finely chopped

1 tbsp vegetable oil

1 tsp ground turmeric

1 tsp ground coriander

1 tsp ground cumin

2 lb 4 oz/1 kg mixed vegetables, such as
   cauliflower, zucchini, potatoes, carrots, and
   green beans, cut into chunks

scant 1 cup coconut cream or coconut milk

salt and pepper

2 tbsp chopped fresh cilantro, to garnish

cooked rice, to serve

1. Put the onion, garlic, ginger, and chiles in a food processor and process until almost smooth.

2. Heat the oil in a large, heavy-bottom pan over low–medium heat, add the onion mixture, and cook, stirring constantly, for 5 minutes.

3. Add the turmeric, coriander, and cumin and cook, stirring frequently, for 3–4 minutes. Add the vegetables and stir to coat in the spice paste.

4. Add the coconut cream to the vegetables, cover, and let simmer for 30–40 minutes, until the vegetables are tender.

5. Season to taste with salt and pepper, garnish with the cilantro, and serve with rice.

Egg Fu Yung

SERVES 4–6

2 eggs

½ tsp salt

pinch of white pepper

1 tsp butter

2 tbsp vegetable or peanut oil

1 tsp finely chopped garlic

1 small onion, finely sliced

1 green bell pepper, finely sliced

2¼ cups cooked rice, chilled

1 tbsp light soy sauce

1 tbsp finely chopped scallion

1 cup bean sprouts

2 drops of sesame oil

1. Beat the eggs with the salt and pepper. Heat the butter in a skillet and pour in the eggs. Cook as an omelet, until set, then remove from the pan and cut into slivers.

2. In a preheated wok or deep pan, heat the oil and stir-fry the garlic until fragrant. Add the onion and stir-fry for 1 minute, then add the bell pepper and stir for an additional minute. Stir in the rice and, when the grains are separated, stir in the soy sauce and cook for 1 minute.

3. Add the scallion and egg strips and stir well, then add the bean sprouts and sesame oil. Stir-fry for 1 minute and serve.

Chengdu Noodles in Sesame Sauce

SERVES 4–6

14 oz/400 g thin wheat flour noodles
1 cup bean sprouts
1 tbsp finely chopped scallion
2 tbsp sesame seeds

SAUCE
1 tbsp sugar
1 tbsp sesame oil
2 oz/55 g sesame paste
1 tbsp chili oil
2 tsp dark soy sauce
1 tbsp black Chinese vinegar

1. Cook the noodles according to the directions on the package. When cooked, rinse under cold water and set aside. Blanch the bean sprouts in a large pan of boiling water for 30 seconds. Drain and set aside.

2. To prepare the sauce, beat all the ingredients together until the sauce is smooth and thick.

3. To serve, toss the noodles in the sauce, stir in the bean sprouts, and sprinkle with the scallion and sesame seeds.

Side Dishes and Desserts

A Chinese meal usually includes an appetizing selection of small dishes, similar to hors d'oeuvres in the West. Typical are tasty meat or vegetables packaged in crisp-fried pastry wrappers—egg rolls or deep-fried wontons, for example—often served with a simple dipping sauce. Shrimp Toasts and spicy Soy Chicken Wings are also popular. A few simple vegetable side dishes, such as Stir-Fried Bean Sprouts or Spicy Green Beans, are also part of a typical meal.

Rice, of course, is an essential and satisfying part of most Chinese meals. Plainly steamed, it provides a complementary texture to other ingredients and absorbs the stronger flavors of well-seasoned meat and fish. Also popular, both at home and in restaurants, is Egg-Fried

Rice. This dish is a good way of using up leftover rice and can be easily transformed into a filling main dish with the addition of a little meat or seafood and some vegetables.

Desserts do not feature largely in China, although at banquets or formal dinners sweet dishes are served to punctuate the long succession of savory dishes. Fresh fruit, either on its own or as part of an impressive fruit salad, might also be served on such occasions. Irresistible Toffee Bananas and Toffee Apple Slices are popular, particularly in Peking, where chefs are adept at caramelizing sugar in hot oil. Sweet dishes are more likely to be eaten separately from a meal as between-meal snacks.

Pork and Shrimp Egg Rolls

MAKES 20–25

6 dried Chinese mushrooms, soaked in warm water for 20 minutes

1 tbsp vegetable or peanut oil, plus extra for deep-frying

8 oz/225 g ground pork

1 tsp dark soy sauce

1 cup fresh or canned bamboo shoots, rinsed and julienned (if using fresh shoots, boil in water first for 30 minutes)

pinch of salt

3½ oz/100 g shrimp, peeled, deveined, and chopped

generous 1½ cups bean sprouts, coarsely chopped

1 tbsp finely chopped scallion

25 egg roll wrappers

1 egg white, lightly beaten

1. Squeeze out any excess water from the mushrooms and finely slice, discarding any tough stems.

2. In a preheated wok or deep pan, heat the tablespoon of oil and stir-fry the pork until it changes color. Add the soy sauce, bamboo shoots, mushrooms, and salt. Stir over high heat for 3 minutes.

3. Add the shrimp and cook for 2 minutes, then add the bean sprouts and cook for an additional minute. Remove from the heat and stir in the scallion. Let cool.

4. Place a tablespoon of the mixture toward the bottom of a wrapper. Roll once to secure the filling, then fold in the sides to create a 4 inch/10 cm long egg roll and continue to roll up. Seal with egg white.

5. Heat enough oil for deep-frying in a wok, deep-fat fryer, or large, heavy-bottom pan to 350–375°F/ 180–190°C, or until a cube of bread browns in 30 seconds. Cook the egg rolls, in batches, for about 5 minutes, until golden brown and crispy.

Vegetarian Egg Rolls

MAKES 20

6 dried Chinese mushrooms, soaked in warm
water for 20 minutes

2 oz/55 g thin rice noodles, soaked in warm
water for 20 minutes

2 tbsp vegetable or peanut oil, plus extra
for greasing

1 tbsp finely chopped fresh ginger

generous ⅔ cup julienned carrot

scant 1 cup finely shredded cabbage

1 tbsp finely sliced scallion

1 tbsp light soy sauce

3 oz/85 g tofu, drained and cut into
small cubes

½ tsp salt

pinch of white pepper

pinch of sugar

20 egg roll wrappers

1 egg white, lightly beaten

dark soy sauce, to serve

1. Squeeze out any excess water from the mushrooms and finely chop, discarding any tough stems.
   Drain the noodles and coarsely chop.

2. In a preheated wok or deep pan, heat the 2 tablespoons of oil, then toss in the ginger and cook
   until fragrant. Add the mushrooms and stir for about 2 minutes. Add the carrot, cabbage, and
   scallion and stir-fry for 1 minute. Add the noodles and light soy sauce and stir-fry for 1 minute. Add
   the tofu and cook for an additional minute. Season with the salt, pepper, and sugar and mix well.
   Continue cooking for 1–2 minutes, or until the carrot has softened. Remove from the heat and let
   the mixture cool.

3. Place a scant tablespoon of the mixture toward the bottom of a wrapper. Roll once to secure the
   filling, then fold in the sides to create a 4 inch/10 cm long egg roll and continue to roll up. Seal with
   egg white.

4. Heat enough oil for deep-frying in a wok, deep-fat fryer, or large, heavy-bottom pan to 350–375°F/
   180–190°C, or until a cube of bread browns in 30 seconds. Without overcrowding the pan, cook the
   rolls for about 5 minutes, or until golden brown and crispy. Serve with dark soy sauce for dipping.

Soy Chicken Wings

SERVES 3–4

9 oz/250 g chicken wings
1 cup water
1 tbsp sliced scallion
1-inch/2.5-cm piece fresh ginger,
    cut into 4 slices

2 tbsp light soy sauce
½ tsp dark soy sauce
1 star anise
1 tsp sugar

1. Wash and dry the chicken wings. Bring the water to a boil in a small pan, then add the chicken, scallion, and ginger and bring back to a boil.

2. Add the remaining ingredients, then cover and simmer for 30 minutes. Meanwhile, preheat the oven to 350°F/180°C.

3. Remove the chicken wings with a slotted spoon and drain on paper towels. Spread out in a single layer in a roasting pan and cook in the preheated oven for 15–20 minutes, until lightly browned. Serve hot.

Shrimp Toasts

MAKES 16

3½ oz/100g shrimp, peeled and deveined

2 egg whites

2 tbsp cornstarch

½ tsp sugar

pinch of salt

2 tbsp finely chopped cilantro leaves

2 slices day-old white bread

vegetable or peanut oil, for deep-frying

1. Pound the shrimp to a paste with a pestle or process briefly in a food processor.

2. Mix the shrimp with 1 of the egg whites and 1 tablespoon of the cornstarch. Add the sugar and salt and stir in the cilantro. Mix the remaining egg white with the remaining cornstarch.

3. Remove the crusts from the bread and cut each slice into 8 triangles. Brush the top of each piece with the egg white-and-cornstarch mixture, then add 1 teaspoon of the shrimp mixture. Smooth the top.

4. Heat enough oil for deep-frying in a wok, deep-fat fryer, or large, heavy-bottom pan to 350–375°F/ 180–190°C, or until a cube of bread browns in 30 seconds. Without overcrowding the wok, cook the toasts, shrimp-side up, for about 2 minutes. Turn and cook for an additional 2 minutes, or until beginning to turn golden brown. Remove with a slotted spoon, drain on paper towels, and serve warm.

Stir-Fried Broccoli

SERVES 4

2 tbsp vegetable oil
2 medium heads of broccoli, cut into florets
2 tbsp light soy sauce
1 tsp cornstarch
1 tbsp superfine sugar

1 tsp grated fresh ginger
1 garlic clove, crushed
pinch of hot chile flakes
1 tsp toasted sesame seeds, to garnish

1. In a large skillet or wok, heat the oil until almost smoking. Stir-fry the broccoli for 4–5 minutes.

2. In a small bowl, combine the soy sauce, cornstarch, sugar, ginger, garlic, and chile flakes. Add the mixture to the broccoli. Cook over a gentle heat, stirring constantly, for 2–3 minutes, until the sauce thickens slightly.

3. Transfer to a serving dish, garnish with the sesame seeds, and serve immediately.

Stir-Fried Bean Sprouts

SERVES 4

1 tbsp vegetable or peanut oil
generous 1½ cups bean sprouts
2 tbsp finely chopped scallion

½ tsp salt
pinch of sugar

1. In a preheated wok or deep pan, heat the oil and stir-fry the bean sprouts with the scallion for about 1 minute. Add the salt and sugar and stir. Serve immediately.

Spicy Green Beans

SERVES 4

generous 1¼ cups green beans, trimmed and
    cut diagonally into 3–4 pieces

2 tbsp vegetable or peanut oil

4 dried chiles, cut into 2–3 pieces

½ tsp Sichuan peppers

1 garlic clove, finely sliced

6 thin slices of fresh ginger

2 scallions, white part only, cut diagonally into
    thin pieces

pinch of sea salt

1. Blanch the beans in a large pan of boiling water for 30 seconds. Drain and set aside.

2. In a preheated wok, heat 1 tablespoon of the oil. Over low heat, stir-fry the beans for about
   5 minutes, or until they are beginning to wrinkle. Remove from the wok and set aside.

3. Add the remaining oil to the wok and stir-fry the chiles and peppers until they are fragrant. Add the
   garlic, ginger, and scallions and stir-fry until they begin to soften. Add the beans and toss to mix,
   then add the sea salt and serve immediately on warmed plates.

Stir-Fried Green Beans with Red Bell Pepper

SERVES 4–6

10 oz/280 g green beans, cut into
  2½-inch/6-cm lengths
1 tbsp vegetable or peanut oil

1 red bell pepper, seeded and thinly sliced
pinch of salt
pinch of sugar

1. Blanch the beans in a large pan of boiling water for 30 seconds. Drain and set aside.

2. In a preheated wok, heat the oil and stir-fry the beans for 1 minute over high heat. Add the bell pepper and stir-fry for an additional minute. Sprinkle the salt and sugar on top and serve.

Hot-and-Sour Cabbage

SERVES 4

1 small head of firm white cabbage

1 tbsp vegetable or peanut oil

10 Sichuan peppers or more, to taste

3 dried chiles, coarsely chopped

½ tsp salt

1 tsp white rice vinegar

dash of sesame oil

pinch of sugar

1. To prepare the cabbage, discard the outer leaves and tough stems. Chop the cabbage into 1¼-inch/ 3-cm squares, breaking up the chunks. Rinse thoroughly in cold water.

2. In a preheated wok, heat the vegetable oil and cook the peppers until fragrant. Stir in the chiles. Add the cabbage, a little at a time, together with the salt, and stir-fry for 2 minutes.

3. Add the vinegar, sesame oil, and sugar and cook for an additional minute, or until the cabbage is tender. Serve immediately on warmed plates.

Steamed White Rice

SERVES 3–4

generous 1 cup long-grain white rice

1. Place the rice in a strainer and wash under cold running water. Drain well.

2. Place the rice in a pan with the same volume of water plus a little extra (the water should just cover the rice). Bring to a boil, then cover and simmer for about 15 minutes.

3. Turn off the heat and let the rice continue to cook in its own steam for about 5 minutes. At this point, the grains should be cooked through but not sticking together. Serve.

Egg-Fried Rice

SERVES 4

2 tbsp vegetable or peanut oil
2 cups cooked rice, chilled

1 egg, well beaten

1. Heat the oil in a preheated wok or deep pan and stir-fry the rice for 1 minute, breaking it down as much as possible into individual grains.

2. Quickly add the egg, stirring to coat each piece of rice. Stir until the egg is cooked and the rice, as far as possible, is in single grains. Serve the rice immediately.

Tea-Scented Eggs

SERVES 6

6 eggs   2 tbsp black tea leaves

1. Bring a pan of water to a boil and cook the eggs for 10 minutes. Remove the eggs from the pan and lightly crack the shells with the back of a spoon.

2. Bring the water back to a boil and simmer the tea leaves for 5 minutes. Turn off the heat. Place the eggs in the tea and let stand until the tea has cooled.

3. Serve the eggs whole for breakfast or as part of a meal.

Pears in Honey Syrup

SERVES 4

4 medium-ripe pears
generous ¾ cup water

1 tsp sugar
1 tbsp honey

1. Peel each pear, leaving the stem intact. Wrap each in aluminum foil and place in a pan with the stems resting on the side of the pan. Add enough water to cover at least half of the height of the pears. Bring to a boil and simmer for 30 minutes. Remove the pears from the pan and carefully remove the aluminum foil, reserving any juices. Set the pears aside to cool.

2. Bring the measured water to a boil. Add any pear juices, the sugar, and honey and boil for 5 minutes. Remove from the heat and let cool a little.

3. To serve, place each pear in a small individual dish. Pour a little syrup over each and serve just warm.

Fresh Fruit Salad with Lemon Juice

SERVES 4–6

2 tbsp sugar

1 lb/450 g mixed melons, peeled, seeded, and cut into balls or cubes

2 bananas, sliced

juice of 1 lemon

1. In a large bowl, sprinkle the sugar over the melon pieces. Toss the banana in the lemon juice and add to the melon, then serve immediately.

Mango Pudding

SERVES 6

1 oz/25 g sago, soaked in water for at least
   20 minutes

1 cup warm water

2 tbsp sugar

1 large, ripe mango, about 10 oz/280 g

generous ¾ cup heavy cream

1 tbsp powdered gelatin, dissolved in 1 cup
   warm water

1. Drain the sago and place in a pan with the warm water. Bring to a boil and then cook over low heat for 10 minutes, stirring frequently until thick. Stir in the sugar and let cool.

2. Peel the mango and slice off the flesh from the pit. Reserving a few small slices for decoration, blend the mango to a smooth paste in a food processor or blender. Stir in the cream and add the gelatin.

3. Add the sago to the mango mixture and mix well. Pour into 6 small bowls and refrigerate until set. Decorate with the reserved mango slices before serving.

Toffee Bananas

SERVES 4

½ cup self-rising flour
1 egg, beaten
5 tbsp ice water
4 large, ripe bananas
3 tbsp lemon juice
2 tbsp rice flour
vegetable oil, for deep-frying

CARAMEL
generous ½ cup superfine sugar
4 tbsp ice water, plus an extra bowl
   of ice water for setting
2 tbsp sesame seeds

1. Sift the self-rising flour into a bowl. Make a well in the center, add the egg and the 5 tablespoons of iced water, and beat from the center outward, until combined into a smooth batter.

2. Peel the bananas and cut into 2-inch/5-cm pieces. Gently shape them into balls with your hands. Brush with lemon juice to prevent discoloration, then roll them in rice flour until coated.

3. Heat enough oil for deep-frying in a wok, deep-fat fryer, or large, heavy-bottom pan to 350–375°F/180–190°C, or until a cube of bread browns in 30 seconds. Coat the balls in the batter and cook, in batches, for about 2 minutes, until golden. Remove with a slotted spoon and drain on paper towels.

4. To make the caramel, put the sugar into a small pan over low heat. Add the 4 tablespoons of ice water and heat, stirring, until the sugar dissolves. Simmer for 5 minutes, remove from the heat, and stir in the sesame seeds. Toss the banana balls in the caramel, scoop them out, and drop into the bowl of ice water to set. Remove with a slotted spoon and divide among individual serving bowls. Serve immediately.

Banana and Coconut Fritters

SERVES 4

½ cup all-purpose flour
2 tbsp rice flour
1 tbsp superfine sugar
1 egg, separated
⅔ cup coconut milk
vegetable oil, for deep-frying
4 large bananas

TO DECORATE/SERVE
1 tsp confectioners' sugar
1 tsp ground cinnamon
lime wedges

1. Sift the all-purpose flour, rice flour, and superfine sugar into a bowl and make a well in the center. Add the egg yolk and coconut milk. Beat the mixture until a smooth, thick batter forms.

2. Beat the egg white in a clean, dry bowl until stiff enough to hold soft peaks. Fold it into the batter lightly and evenly.

3. Heat enough oil for deep-frying in a wok, deep-fat fryer, or large, heavy-bottom pan to 350–375°F/ 180–190°C, or until a cube of bread browns in 30 seconds. Cut the bananas in half, first lengthwise and then crosswise, then dip them quickly into the batter to coat them.

4. Drop the bananas carefully into the hot oil and deep-fry, in batches, for 2–3 minutes, until golden brown, turning once.

5. Remove with a slotted spoon and drain on paper towels. Sprinkle with confectioners' sugar and cinnamon and serve immediately with lime wedges for squeezing over.

Toffee Apple Slices

SERVES 6

4 apples, peeled, cored, and each cut into
   8 wedges
vegetable or peanut oil, for deep-frying

BATTER
⅔ cup all-purpose flour
1 egg, beaten
½ cup cold water

TOFFEE SYRUP
4 tbsp sesame oil
scant 1¼ cups sugar
2 tbsp sesame seeds, toasted

1. To prepare the batter, sift the flour into a bowl and stir in the egg. Slowly add the water, beating to give a smooth, thick batter. Dip each apple wedge into the batter.

2. Heat enough oil for deep-frying in a wok, deep-fat fryer, or large, heavy-bottom pan to 350–375°F/180–190°C, or until a cube of bread browns in 30 seconds. Deep-fry the apple wedges until golden brown. Drain on paper towels and set aside.

3. To make the toffee syrup, heat the sesame oil in a small, heavy-bottom pan and when beginning to smoke add the sugar, stirring constantly, until the mixture caramelizes and turns golden. Remove from the heat, then stir in the sesame seeds and pour into a large skillet.

4. Over low heat, place the apple wedges in the syrup, turning once. When coated, drop each wedge into a bowl of ice water to set. Remove with a slotted spoon and serve immediately.

Almond Dessert in Ginger Sauce

SERVES 6–8

3¾ cups water
⅛ oz/5 g agar
scant 1¼ cups sugar
½ cup evaporated milk
1 tsp almond extract

GINGER SAUCE
2½-inch/6-cm piece fresh ginger,
  coarsely chopped
3¾ cups water
generous ¼ cup light brown sugar

1. Bring the water to a boil in a pan. Add the agar and stir until dissolved. Stir in the sugar.

2. Pour through a strainer into a shallow dish. Pour in the evaporated milk, stirring constantly. When slightly cooled, stir in the almond extract. Let chill in the refrigerator until set.

3. To make the ginger sauce, boil the ginger, water, and brown sugar in a pan, covered, for at least 1½ hours, or until the sauce is golden in color. Discard the ginger.

4. Using a sharp knife, cut the almond dessert into thin slices and arrange in individual bowls. Pour over a little ginger sauce, warm or cold, and serve.

Index